D1508958

201
BROWNIES
and Bars

Published by
Black Dog & Leventhal Publishers, Inc.
151 West 19th Street
New York, NY 10011

Distributed by
Workman Publishing Company
708 Broadway
New York, NY 10003

Manufactured in The United Kingdom

Gillespie, Gregg R., 1934–
201 brownies & bars : chewy, crumbly, crunchy cakes : 201 delicious recipes, 201 tantalizing pictures / by Gregg R. Gillespie.
p. cm.

ISBN: 1-57912-117-9
1. Brownies (Cookery) I. Title
TX772.G52 2000
641.8'654--dc21

j i h g f e d c b

201
BROWNIES
and Bars

Chewy, Crumbly, Crunchy Cakes

201 Delicious Recipes
201 Tantalizing Pictures

BY GREGG R. GILLESPIE

BLACK DOG
& LEVENTHAL
PUBLISHERS
NEW YORK

TABLE OF CONTENTS

ALMOND AWARDS

Bar Cookies

YIELD: *1 to 2 dozen*
TOTAL TIME: *50 minutes*

CRUST
1 cup all-purpose flour
½ teaspoon salt
½ cup vegetable shortening
½ cup granulated sugar
1 tablespoon grated lemon zest

TOPPING
½ cup vegetable shortening
½ cup granulated sugar
1 cup heavy cream
1 cup almonds, ground

1 Preheat the oven to 375 degrees. Lightly grease an 11 by 7-inch baking pan.

2 To make the crust, combine the flour and salt.

3 In a large bowl, cream the shortening and sugar. Beat in the lemon zest. Gradually blend in the dry ingredients.

4 Press the dough evenly over the bottom of the prepared baking pan. Bake for 12 minutes. Transfer pan to wire rack to cool slightly.

5 Meanwhile, make the topping: Melt the shortening in a small saucepan. Stir in the sugar, cream, and almonds.

6 Spread the almond topping over the warm crust. Bake for 20 minutes longer, or until firm to the touch.

7 Cool in the pan on a wire rack before cutting into large or small bars.

ALMOND BARS

Bar Cookies

YIELD: *2 to 3 dozen*
TOTAL TIME: *35 minutes*

½ cup all-purpose flour
¼ teaspoon baking powder
2 large eggs, separated
Pinch of salt
1 cup packed light brown sugar
1 teaspoon vanilla extract
⅓ cup butter, at room temperature
1 cup almonds, ground
Powdered sugar for dusting

1 Preheat the oven to 350 degrees. Lightly grease and flour a 9-inch square baking pan.

2 Combine the flour and baking powder.

3 In a large bowl, beat the egg whites with the salt until foamy. Gradually beat in the brown sugar. Beat in the vanilla extract. Blend in the flour mixture.

4 In another bowl, beat the egg yolks and butter until well blended.

5 Gradually fold the butter mixture into the egg-white mixture. Fold in the almonds.

6 Press the dough evenly into the prepared pan. Bake for 20 to 25 minutes, or until the top is a golden brown. Cool in the pan on a wire rack.

7 Dust with powdered sugar and cut into large or small bars.

Baking notes: If you like, drizzle white sugar icing over the top of these cookies in a crisscross pattern before cutting them into bars. For a festive look, use a colored icing and cut the bars into bite-sized pieces.

ALMOND BUTTER COOKIES

Rolled Cookies

Yield: 2½ dozen
Total time: 45 minutes

1¼ cups all-purpose flour
¼ cup granulated sugar
¾ cup butter
1 teaspoon almond extract
⅛ teaspoon salt
1 large egg white, lightly beaten

TOPPING
¼ cup granulated sugar
1 tablespoon finely ground toasted almonds
⅛ teaspoon ground cinnamon

1 In large bowl, beat together the flour, sugar, butter, almond extract, and salt. The dough will be crumbly. Cover and chill for at least 4 hours.

2 Preheat the oven to 350 degrees.

3 On a floured surface, roll out the dough to a 12 by 8-inch rectangle. Cut lengthwise into 1-inch-wide strips. Then cut each strip into 4 pieces and place 1 inch apart on ungreased baking sheets.

4 Brush the tops of the cookies with the beaten egg white. Let stand for 20 minutes.

5 To make the topping, combine all of the ingredients in a small bowl. Sprinkle evenly over the cookies.

6 Bake for 10 to 12 minutes, or until the cookies are very light brown. Transfer to wire racks to cool.

Baking notes: For a different texture, coarsely grind the almonds for the topping. Sprinkle on the sugar and cinnamon, then sprinkle on the almonds.

ALMOND ROCA COOKIES

Bar Cookies

Yield: 1 to 2 dozen
Total time: 35 minutes

1 cup vegetable shortening
½ cup granulated sugar
1 large egg yolk
1 teaspoon almond extract
2 cups all-purpose flour
10 ounces milk chocolate (see Baking notes), chopped
½ cup almonds, sliced

1 Preheat the oven to 350 degrees. Grease a 15 by 10-inch baking pan.

2 In a large bowl, cream the vegetable shortening and sugar. Beat in the egg yolk and almond extract. Blend in the flour.

3 Spread the dough evenly in the prepared pan. Bake for 18 to 20 minutes, until lightly colored.

4 Meanwhile, melt the chocolate in a double boiler over low heat, stirring until smooth. Remove from the heat.

5 Spread the melted chocolate over the top of the warm cookies. Sprinkle with the almonds. Let cool in the pan on a rack before cutting into large or small bars.

Baking notes: Do not use melted candy bars; use only baker's-style milk chocolate.

ALMOND-COFFEE DELIGHTS

Bar Cookies

YIELD: *1 to 3 dozen*
TOTAL TIME: *50 minutes*

CRUST
½ cup butter
3 tablespoons powdered sugar
2 large egg yolks
1 teaspoon instant coffee granules
1 tablespoon warm water
2 cups all-purpose flour, or more if needed

FILLING
½ cup semisweet chocolate chips
2 large egg whites
Pinch of salt
¼ cup granulated sugar
¼ cup almonds, ground
¼ cup almonds, chopped

1 Preheat the oven to 350 degrees. Lightly grease a 9-inch square baking pan.

2 To make the crust, combine the butter, powdered sugar, egg yolks, coffee, and water in a large bowl and beat until smooth. Blend in the flour. The mixture should be crumbly. If necessary, add a little more flour.

3 Press the mixture evenly over the bottom of the prepared pan. Bake for 20 minutes.

4 Meanwhile, make the filling: Melt the chocolate chips in a double boiler over low heat, stirring until smooth. Let cool slightly.

5 In a large bowl, beat the egg whites with the salt until frothy. Gradually beat in the sugar and beat until stiff peaks form. Fold in the melted chocolate. Fold in the almonds.

6 Spread the filling over the hot crust. Sprinkle the chopped almonds over the top. Bake for 20 minutes longer, until topping is set. Cool in the pan on a rack before cutting into large or small bars.

Almond Squares

Bar Cookies

Yield: 1 to 2 dozen
Total time: 60 minutes

1 cup vegetable shortening
1 cup granulated sugar
1 large egg, separated
½ teaspoon almond extract
¼ teaspoon salt
2 cups all-purpose flour
1½ cups sliced almonds

1 Preheat the oven to 325 degrees.

2 In a large bowl, cream the vegetable shortening and sugar. Beat in the egg yolk and almond extract. Beat in the salt. Gradually blend in the flour. The dough will be stiff.

3 Spread the dough evenly in an ungreased 9-inch baking pan.

4 In a medium bowl, beat the egg white until stiff but not dry. Spread evenly over the cookie dough. Sprinkle with the almonds.

5 Bake for 40 minutes, until the top is lightly colored. Let cool in the pan on a rack before cutting into large or small bars.

Baking notes: For variation, spread your favorite fruit preserves over the unbaked crust, then spread the beaten egg white over the fruit. Bake for 30 to 35 minutes.

Ambrosia Bars

Bar Cookies

Yield: 2 to 3 dozen
Total time: 35 minutes

2 cups all-purpose flour
½ teaspoon baking powder
½ teaspoon baking soda
¼ teaspoon salt
¾ cup vegetable shortening
1 cup packed light brown sugar
1 large egg
¼ cup fresh orange juice
1 tablespoon grated orange zest
1 cup (6 ounces) butterscotch chips
1 cup shredded coconut

1 Preheat the oven to 350 degrees. Grease a 13 by 9-inch baking pan.

2 Combine the flour, baking powder, baking soda, and salt.

3 In a large bowl, cream the vegetable shortening and brown sugar. Beat in the egg, orange juice, and zest. Gradually blend in the dry ingredients. Fold in the butterscotch chips and coconut.

4 Spread the batter evenly in the prepared pan.

5 Bake for 25 to 30 minutes, or until the top is a golden brown. Cool in the pan on a rack before cutting into large or small squares.

Apple Bars

Bar Cookies

YIELD: *1 to 2 dozen*
TOTAL TIME: *50 minutes*

¾ cup all-purpose flour
½ teaspoon baking powder
¼ teaspoon baking soda
½ teaspoon ground ginger
¼ teaspoon ground nutmeg
⅓ cup vegetable shortening
¾ cup granulated sugar
2 large eggs
1 cup diced, peeled apples

TOPPING
1½ teaspoons granulated sugar
½ teaspoon ground cinnamon

1 Preheat the oven to 350 degrees.

2 Combine the flour, baking powder, baking soda, ginger, and nutmeg.

3 In a large bowl, cream the vegetable shortening and sugar. Beat in the eggs. Gradually blend in the dry ingredients. Fold in the apples.

4 Spread the dough evenly in an ungreased 9-inch square baking pan.

5 Combine the cinnamon and sugar for the topping. Sprinkle evenly over the dough.

6 Bake for 25 to 30 minutes, or until firm to the touch. Let cool in the pan on a rack before cutting into large or small bars.

Baking notes: Add ½ cup raisins and/or ½ cup chopped nuts to the dough if desired. Drizzle white icing over the top as soon as the bars are baked. (See Pantry.)

Apple Butter-Oatmeal Bars

Bar Cookies

YIELD: *2 to 3 dozen*
TOTAL TIME: *30 minutes*

⅔ cup all-purpose flour
½ teaspoon baking powder
¼ teaspoon salt
½ cup vegetable shortening
½ cup apple butter
½ cup packed dark brown sugar
1 large egg
½ teaspoon baking soda
1 tablespoon warm water
1 cup rolled oats
1 cup flaked coconut (optional)

1 Preheat the oven to 350 degrees. Grease a 13 by 9-inch baking pan.

2 Combine the flour, baking powder and salt.

3 In a large bowl, cream the vegetable shortening, apple butter, and brown sugar. Beat in the egg.

4 Dissolve the baking soda in the warm water and add to the creamed mixture, beating until smooth. Gradually blend in the dry ingredients. Fold in the oats coconut.

5 Spread the mixture evenly in the prepared pan.

6 Bake for 15 to 20 minutes, or until lightly colored. Cool in the pan on a rack before cutting into large or small bars.

Baking notes: If you like chocolate, add chocolate chips to the dough and drizzle melted chocolate over the top of the cooled cookies.

Apple-Spice Bars

Bar Cookies

YIELD: *1 to 2 dozen*
TOTAL TIME: *55 minutes*

1½ cups all-purpose flour
½ teaspoon baking powder
½ teaspoon ground nutmeg
½ teaspoon ground ginger
¼ teaspoon salt
⅔ cup vegetable shortening
1½ cups granulated sugar
4 large eggs
½ teaspoon baking soda
1 tablespoon warm water
1 cup diced, peeled apples

TOPPING
¼ cup granulated sugar
1 teaspoon ground cinnamon

1 Preheat the oven to 350 degrees. Grease a 13 by 9-inch baking pan.

2 Combine the flour, baking powder, spices, and salt.

3 In a large bowl, cream the vegetable shortening and sugar. Beat in the eggs.

4 Dissolve the baking soda in the warm water and add to the egg mixture, beating until smooth. Gradually blend in the dry ingredients. Fold in the apples.

5 Spread the mixture evenly in the prepared pan. Combine the sugar and cinnamon for the topping and sprinkle evenly over the cookies.

6 Bake for 25 to 30 minutes, or until top is lightly browned. Cool in the pan on a rack before cutting into large or small bars.

Applesauce Brownies

Bar Cookies

YIELD: *1 to 2 dozen*
TOTAL TIME: *40 minutes*

2 ounces semisweet chocolate, chopped
1 cup all-purpose flour
1 teaspoon baking powder
½ teaspoon ground cinnamon
¼ teaspoon salt
½ cup vegetable shortening
1¼ cups granulated sugar
2 large eggs
1 teaspoon vanilla extract
½ cup unsweetened applesauce, at room temperature
½ cup walnuts, chopped

1 Preheat the oven to 350 degrees. Grease a 13 by 9-inch baking pan.

2 Melt the chocolate in a double boiler over low heat, stirring until smooth. Let cool.

3 Combine the flour, baking powder, cinnamon, and salt.

4 In a large bowl, cream the vegetable shortening and sugar. Beat in the eggs one at a time.

5 In a medium bowl, combine the applesauce, melted chocolate, and vanilla extract. Add to the egg mixture, beating until smooth. Gradually blend in the dry ingredients. Fold in the nuts.

6 Spread the mixture evenly in the prepared pan.

7 Bake for 20 to 25 minutes, or until a toothpick inserted in the center comes out clean. Cool in the pan on a rack before cutting into large or small bars.

Baking notes: For variation, substitute almond extract for the vanilla extract and almonds, chopped for the walnuts.

Applesauce Date Bars

Bar Cookies

Yield: *2 to 3 dozen*
Total time: *45 minutes*

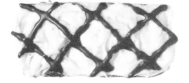

2 cups all-purpose flour
1 teaspoon ground cinnamon
½ teaspoon ground cardamom
Pinch of salt
¾ cup vegetable shortening
1 cup granulated sugar
2 teaspoons baking soda
1 tablespoon warm water
2 large eggs
2 cups unsweetened applesauce
1 cup pitted dates, chopped
1 cup walnuts, chopped

1 Preheat the oven to 350 degrees. Grease a 13 by 9-inch baking pan.

2 Combine the flour, cinnamon, cardamom, and salt.

3 In a large bowl, cream the vegetable shortening and sugar.

4 Dissolve the baking soda in the warm water and add to the creamed mixture, beating until smooth. Beat in the eggs. Beat in the applesauce. Gradually blend in the dry ingredients. Fold in the dates and walnuts.

5 Spread the mixture evenly in the prepared pan.

6 Bake for 25 to 30 minutes, or until golden brown on top. Cool in the pan on a rack before cutting into large or small bars.

Baking notes: For a decorative touch, frost these with Vanilla Icing (see Pantry), and drizzle Dark Chocolate Icing (see Pantry) over the top.

Apricot Bars I

Bar Cookies

Yield: *2 to 3 dozen*
Total time: *45 minutes*

1¾ cups all-purpose flour
½ cup almonds, ground fine
½ teaspoon salt
¾ cup vegetable shortening
¾ cup powdered sugar
½ teaspoon almond extract

Filling
One 12-ounce jar apricot preserves
½ cup glacé cherries, diced
1½ teaspoons brandy

1 Preheat the oven to 350 degrees.

2 Combine the flour, almonds, and salt.

3 In a large bowl, cream the vegetable shortening and powdered sugar. Beat in the almond extract. Gradually blend in the dry ingredients.

4 Set aside 1 cup of the almond mixture for the topping. Spread the remaining mixture evenly over the bottom of an ungreased 13 by 9-inch baking pan.

5 To make the filling, combine the apricot preserves, cherries, and brandy in a small bowl, and stir until well blended. Spread the filling evenly over the almond mixture. Crumble the reserved almond mixture over the filling.

6 Bake for 30 to 35 minutes, until the edges are dark golden brown. Cut into large or small bars while still warm, and cool in the pan on a rack.

APPLE STRIPS

Bar Cookies

YIELD: *3 to 4 dozen*
TOTAL TIME: *45 minutes*
CHILLING TIME: *2 hours*

CRUST
2 cups all-purpose flour
¼ cup granulated sugar
¾ cup vegetable shortening
3 tablespoons sour cream
½ teaspoon grated lemon zest

FILLING
5 medium apples, peeled, cored and
  sliced thin
½ cup granulated sugar
1 tablespoon raisins
1 large egg yolk, beaten
Powdered sugar for sprinkling

1 To make the crust, combine the flour and sugar in a bowl. Cut in the vegetable shortening until the mixture resembles coarse crumbs. Stir in the sour cream and lemon zest.

2 Divide the dough in half. Wrap in waxed paper and let chill for 2 hours.

3 Preheat the oven to 325 degrees.

4 On a lightly floured surface, roll out half of the dough to a 9-inch square. Fit the dough into an ungreased 9-inch square baking pan.

5 To make filling, layer the apples evenly over the crust. Sprinkle the sugar and the raisins on top.

6 Roll out the remaining dough to a 9-inch square. Cut into 1-inch-wide strips and arrange in a lattice pattern over the filling. Brush the lattice strips with the beaten egg yolk.

7 Bake for 18 to 20 minutes, or until the crust is golden brown. Sprinkle powdered sugar over the warm cookies, and cut into 2 by 1-inch strips.

Baking notes: Shredded coconut may be added to the crust for a different flavor and texture.

Apricot Bars II

Bar Cookies

YIELD: *2 to 3 dozen*
TOTAL TIME: *75 minutes*

Filling
⅔ cup dried apricots
⅓ cup all-purpose flour
½ teaspoon baking powder
¼ teaspoon salt
½ cup walnuts, chopped
1½ cups packed light brown sugar
2 large eggs
½ teaspoon vanilla extract

Crust
1 cup all-purpose flour
¼ cup granulated sugar
½ cup vegetable shortening
Powdered sugar for sprinkling

1 Preheat the oven to 350 degrees. Lightly grease an 8-inch square baking pan.

2 Combine the apricots and ⅓ cup water in a small saucepan. Cover and bring to a boil over medium heat. Cook for 15 minutes, or until soft. Drain and let cool, then chop fine. Set aside.

3 To make the crust, combine the flour and sugar in a bowl. Cut in the vegetable shortening until the mixture resembles coarse crumbs.

4 Press the mixture evenly into the bottom of the prepared pan. Bake for 25 minutes.

5 Meanwhile, make the filling: Combine the flour, baking powder, and salt. Add the walnuts and apricots.

6 In a medium bowl, beat the brown sugar, eggs, and vanilla extract together until thick. Gradually blend in the dry ingredients.

7 Spread the apricot mixture evenly over the warm crust. Bake for 25 minutes longer, until filling is set.

8 Cool in the pan on a rack before cutting into large or small bars. Sprinkle with powdered sugar.

Apricot Bars III

Bar Cookies

Yield: *2 to 4 dozen*
Total time: *40 minutes*

2 cups all-purpose flour
2 teaspoons baking powder
½ teaspoon ground nutmeg
½ teaspoon salt
2 teaspoons grated orange zest
4 large eggs
2 cups granulated sugar
1½ cups dried apricots, diced
1 cup walnuts, chopped
Powdered sugar for sprinkling

1 Preheat the oven to 350 degrees. Grease a 13 by 9-inch baking pan.

2 Sift the flour, baking powder, nutmeg, and salt into a bowl. Stir in the orange zest.

3 In a large bowl, beat the eggs and sugar until thick and light-colored. Gradually blend in the dry ingredients. Fold in the apricots and walnuts.

4 Spread the batter evenly in the prepared pan. Bake for 15 to 20 minutes, until the top is golden, and a toothpick inserted into the center comes out clean.

5 Cool in the pan on a rack before cutting into large or small bars. Sprinkle with powdered sugar.

Apricot-Pecan Gems

Bar Cookies

Yield: *1 to 3 dozen*
Total time: *40 minutes*

1 cup dried apricots, diced
1½ cups all-purpose flour
1 teaspoon baking powder
¼ teaspoon salt
½ cup vegetable shortening
1 cup granulated sugar
½ cup packed light brown sugar
2 large eggs
½ cup buttermilk
¼ teaspoon grated orange zest
1 teaspoon baking soda
1 tablespoon warm water
1 cup pecans, chopped
Powdered sugar for sprinkling

1 Preheat the oven to 350 degrees. Grease a 10-inch square baking pan.

2 Place the apricots in a small bowl and add boiling water to cover. Set aside and let soften for 10 minutes.

3 Combine the flour, baking powder, and salt.

4 In a large bowl, cream the vegetable shortening, granulated sugar, and brown sugar. Beat in the eggs and buttermilk. Beat in the orange zest.

5 Dissolve the baking soda in the warm water and add to the buttermilk mixture, beating until smooth. Gradually blend in the dry ingredients.

6 Drain the apricots and fold into the dough. Fold in the nuts.

7 Spread the dough evenly in the prepared pan. Bake for 20 to 25 minutes, until the top is golden.

8 Cool in the pan on a rack. Sprinkle with powdered sugar and cut into large or small bars.

BAKLAVA

Bar Cookies

YIELD: *1 to 4 dozen*
TOTAL TIME: *75 minutes*

1 pound unsalted butter (see Baking note)
½ pound phyllo dough, thawed if frozen
2 cups pecans, chopped
1 to 2 tablespoons whole cloves
⅓ cup granulated sugar
3 cups water
1 cinnamon stick
1 cup honey

1 Preheat the oven to 450 degrees.

2 Melt the butter in a small saucepan.

3 Pour 2 tablespoons of the butter into the bottom of a 13 by 9-inch baking pan. Layer 3 sheets of phyllo dough in the pan, trimming them to fit. Sprinkle about 2 tablespoons of the pecans over the phyllo. Top with 3 more sheets of phyllo and sprinkle with pecans. Continue layering until the pan is three-quarters full. (Do not sprinkle nuts over the top sheet.)

4 Using a sharp knife, score the phyllo to form diamonds. Press a clove into the pointed ends of each diamond. Gradually pour the remaining melted butter over the pastry.

5 Bake for 45 to 50 minutes, until the phyllo is golden brown.

6 Meanwhile, combine the sugar, water, and cinnamon stick in a medium saucepan and bring to a boil, stirring until the sugar dissolves. Lower the heat and simmer for 10 minutes. Add the honey and simmer for 2 minutes longer. Remove from the heat and remove and discard the cinnamon stick.

7 Pour the honey mixture over the hot baklava. Cool in the pan on a rack before cutting into diamonds.

Baking notes: You must use unsalted (sweet) butter for this recipe. Phyllo, or filo, dough is also known as strudel leaves. It can be purchased in specialty stores and many supermarkets. If you like honey, you will like baklava.

BAKED CHEESECAKE BARS

Bar Cookies

YIELD: 1 to 2 dozen
TOTAL TIME: 40 minutes

CRUST
1 cup all-purpose flour
⅓ cup packed light brown sugar
⅓ cup vegetable shortening

FILLING
2 large eggs
1 pound cream cheese, at room temperature
½ cup granulated sugar
2 tablespoons fresh lemon juice
1 tablespoon marsala

1 Preheat the oven to 350 degrees.

2 To make the crust, combine the flour and brown sugar in a bowl. Cut in the vegetable shortening until the mixture resembles coarse crumbs.

3 Press the mixture evenly into the bottom of a 9-inch square baking pan. Bake for 15 minutes.

4 Meanwhile, make the filling: In a large bowl, beat the eggs until thick and light-colored. Beat in the cream cheese and sugar until smooth. Beat in the lemon juice and marsala.

5 Spread the filling evenly over the warm crust. Bake for 20 minutes longer, or until firm to the touch.

6 Cool in the pan on a rack before cutting into large or small bars.

Baking notes: A teaspoon of almond extract can be used in place of the marsala.

BANANA BARS

Bar Cookies

YIELD: 1 to 2 dozen
TOTAL TIME: 40 minutes

1½ cups all-purpose flour
1½ teaspoons baking powder
½ teaspoon salt
¼ cup vegetable shortening
1 cup packed light brown sugar
2 to 3 bananas, mashed
½ teaspoon pineapple juice
½ teaspoon vanilla extract
½ cup walnuts, chopped

TOPPING
⅓ cup powdered sugar
1 teaspoon ground cinnamon

1 Preheat the oven to 350 degrees. Grease a 13 by 9-inch baking pan.

2 Combine the flour, baking powder, and salt.

3 In a large bowl, cream the vegetable shortening and brown sugar. Beat in the bananas, pineapple juice, and vanilla extract. Gradually blend in the dry ingredients. Fold in the nuts.

4 Spread the batter evenly in the prepared pan. Bake for 30 to 35 minutes, until firm to the touch.

5 Combine the powdered sugar and cinnamon for the topping, and sprinkle over the warm cookies. Cut into large or small bars and cool in pans on wire racks.

BANANA-CHIP BARS

Bar Cookies

YIELD: *1 to 2 dozen*
TOTAL TIME: *40 minutes*

2 cups all-purpose flour
2 teaspoons baking powder
½ teaspoon salt
¾ cup vegetable shortening
1 cup granulated sugar
¼ cup packed light brown sugar
1 large egg
1 teaspoon vanilla extract
1 cup mashed bananas
1 cup (6 ounces) semisweet chocolate chips

1 Preheat the oven to 350 degrees. Grease a 13 by 9-inch baking pan.

2 Combine the flour, baking powder, and salt.

3 In a large bowl, cream the vegetable shortening and both sugars. Beat in the egg and vanilla extract. Beat in the bananas. Gradually blend in the dry ingredients. Fold in the chocolate chips.

4 Spread the mixture evenly in the prepared pan.

5 Bake for 25 to 30 minutes, until golden brown on top. Cool in the pan on a rack before cutting into large or small bars.

Baking notes: A packaged banana cream frosting goes very well with these bars.

BANANA-COCONUT BARS

Bar Cookies

YIELD: *2 to 3 dozen*
TOTAL TIME: *30 minutes*

1¾ cups all-purpose flour
2 teaspoons baking powder
1 teaspoon baking soda
⅓ cup vegetable shortening
2 to 3 medium bananas, mashed
1 large egg
½ cup milk
¼ teaspoon fresh lemon juice
1½ cups flaked coconut

1 Preheat the oven to 350 degrees. Grease a 13 by 9-inch baking pan.

2 Combine the flour, baking powder, and baking soda.

3 In a large bowl, beat the vegetable shortening and bananas until smooth. Beat in the egg, milk, and lemon juice. Gradually blend in the dry ingredients. Fold in 1 cup of the coconut.

4 Spread the mixture evenly in the prepared pan. Sprinkle the remaining ½ cup coconut over the top.

5 Bake for 15 to 20 minutes, until the top is lightly colored, and a toothpick inserted into the center comes out clean. Cool in the pan on a rack before cutting into large or small bars.

Basic Fudge Brownies

Bar Cookies

Yield: 1 to 2 dozen
Total time: 30 minutes

½ cup plus 2 tablespoons vegetable shortening
2 tablespoons unsweetened cocoa powder
1 cup granulated sugar
2 large eggs
1 teaspoon vanilla extract
½ cup all-purpose flour

1 Preheat the oven to 350 degrees. Grease a 9-inch square baking pan.

2 Combine the vegetable shortening and cocoa in the top of a double boiler and heat over low heat, stirring occasionally, until the shortening is melted.

3 Remove from the heat and stir in the sugar. Stir in the eggs and vanilla extract until well blended. Stir in the flour.

4 Spread the mixture evenly in the prepared pan.

5 Bake for 18 to 20 minutes, until a toothpick inserted in the center comes out clean. Cool in the pan on a rack before cutting into large or small bars.

Baking notes: When cool, these can be spread with chocolate glaze and sprinkled with chopped walnuts before being cut into bars.

Belgian Christmas Cookies

Bar Cookies

Yield: 1 to 2 dozen
Total time: 25 minutes

1⅔ cups all-purpose flour
1½ teaspoons baking powder
½ teaspoon salt
⅔ cup vegetable shortening
1 cup packed light brown sugar
2 large eggs
1 teaspoon almond extract
½ cup walnuts, chopped
½ teaspoon ground cinnamon
Red and green sugar crystals for sprinkling

1 Preheat the oven to 375 degrees.

2 Combine the flour, baking powder, and salt.

3 In a large bowl, cream the vegetable shortening and brown sugar. Beat in the eggs and almond extract. Gradually blend in the dry ingredients.

4 Spread the mixture evenly in an ungreased 13 by 9-inch baking pan. Sprinkle the walnuts and cinnamon over the top. Sprinkle with the colored sugar.

5 Bake for 10 to 12 minutes, until lightly colored. Cut into large or small bars while still warm and cool in the pan on a wire rack.

Baking notes: Use your favorite nuts in these cookies. A tablespoon or so of chopped candied fruit added to the dough will make the cookies even more festive.

Big Orange Bars

Bar Cookies

YIELD: *1 to 3 dozen*
TOTAL TIME: *60 minutes*

CRUST
1 cup all-purpose flour
½ cup powdered sugar
6 tablespoons butter, at room
temperature
1 tablespoon heavy cream

TOPPING
4 large eggs
1¼ cups powdered sugar
6 tablespoons fresh orange juice
2 tablespoons fresh lemon juice
3 tablespoons grated orange zest

1 Preheat the oven to 350
degrees. Grease a 13 by 9-inch
baking pan.

2 To make the crust, combine the
flour and powdered sugar in a
bowl. Cut in the butter until the
mixture resembles coarse
crumbs. Blend in the cream.

3 Press the mixture evenly into
the bottom of the prepared pan.
Bake for 20 minutes.

4 Meanwhile, make the topping:
In a large bowl, beat the eggs
until thick and light-colored. Beat
in the powdered sugar. Beat in
the orange juice and lemon juice.
Fold in the orange zest.

5 Pour the topping mixture over
the warm crust. Bake for 25 to 30
minutes longer, until the topping
is set.

6 Cool in the pan on a rack
before cutting into large or small
bars.

Baking notes: These can be gar-
nished with thin slices of sweet
oranges.

Bittersweet Brownies

Bar Cookies

YIELD: *1 to 3 dozen*
TOTAL TIME: *35 minutes*

2 ounces unsweetened chocolate,
chopped
½ cup all-purpose flour
1 teaspoon baking soda
¼ teaspoon salt
½ cup vegetable shortening
¾ cup granulated sugar
2 large eggs
1 teaspoon vanilla extract
1½ cups pecans, chopped

1 Preheat the oven to 350
degrees. Grease a 9-inch square
baking pan.

2 Melt the chocolate in a double
boiler over low heat, stirring
until smooth. Remove from the
heat.

3 Combine the flour, baking
powder, and salt.

4 In a large bowl, cream the vegetable shortening and sugar. Beat
in the eggs and vanilla extract.
Beat in the melted chocolate.
Gradually blend in the dry ingredients. Stir in the pecans.

5 Spread the mixture evenly in
the prepared pan.

6 Bake for 20 to 25 minutes, until
a toothpick inserted in the center
comes out clean. Cool in the pan
on a rack.

7 Frost with chocolate frosting
and cut into large or small bars.

BLACKBERRY MERINGUE BARS

Bar Cookies

YIELD: *3 to 4 dozen*
TOTAL TIME: *45 minutes*

CRUST
¾ cup vegetable shortening
¼ cup granulated sugar
2 large egg yolks
1½ cups all-purpose flour

TOPPING
2 large egg whites
½ cup granulated sugar
1 cup almonds, chopped
1 cup blackberry puree, unstrained
1 cup shaved fresh coconut (see Baking notes)

1 Preheat the oven to 350 degrees.

2 To make the crust, in a large bowl, cream the vegetable shortening and sugar. Beat in the egg yolks. Gradually blend in the flour.

3 Spread the mixture evenly in the bottom of an ungreased 13 by 9-inch baking pan. Bake for 15 minutes.

4 Meanwhile, make the topping: In a medium bowl, beat the egg whites into stiff peaks. Beat in the sugar. Fold in the nuts.

5 Spread the blackberry puree over the warm crust. Sprinkle with the coconut. Spread the meringue evenly over the top.

6 Bake for 20 to 25 minutes longer, until the topping is set. Cool in the pan on a rack before cutting into large or small bars.

Baking notes: The blackberry puree can be fresh, canned, frozen, preserved, or a compote. If you do not have fresh coconut available packaged flaked coconut can be used. These cookies can be made with almost any type of berry. If desired, add ¼ teaspoon almond extract to the crust for subtle flavor.

BLITZKUCHEN

Bar Cookies

YIELD: *1 to 2 dozen*
TOTAL TIME: *45 minutes*

CRUST
1 cup vegetable shortening
1 cup granulated sugar
2 large eggs, separated
3 cups flour
½ teaspoon salt

TOPPING
2 large egg whites
½ cup almonds, ground fine
¾ teaspoon ground cinnamon
¼ teaspoon granulated sugar

1 Preheat the oven to 350 degrees.

2 To make the crust, cream the vegetable shortening and sugar in a large bowl. Combine flour and salt and add. Beat in the egg yolks.

3 In another bowl, beat the egg whites with the salt until they hold stiff peaks. Fold the egg whites into the egg yolk mixture. Gradually fold in the flour.

4 Press the mixture evenly into the bottom of an ungreased 8-inch square baking pan.

5 To make the topping: In a medium bowl, beat the egg whites until stiff but not dry. Fold in the ground almonds, then fold in the cinnamon and sugar.

6 Spread the topping evenly over the prepared crust.

7 Bake for 25 to 30 minutes, until firm to the touch. Cool in the pan on a rack before cutting into large or small bars.

BLOND BROWNIES

Bar Cookies

YIELD: *1 to 2 dozen*
TOTAL TIME: *30 minutes*

½ cup butter, at room temperature
2 cups packed light brown sugar
4 large eggs
2 teaspoons almond extract
2½ cups all-purpose flour
2 teaspoons baking powder
1½ cups almonds, chopped
1½ cups (9 ounces) semisweet
   chocolate chips

1 Preheat the oven to 375
degrees.

2 In a large bowl, cream the butter and brown sugar. Beat in the
eggs and almond extract. Gradually blend in the flour and baking
powder. Stir in the almonds and
chocolate chips.

3 Spread the batter evenly in an
ungreased 13 by 9-inch baking
pan.

4 Bake for 15 to 20 minutes, until
a toothpick inserted in the center
comes out clean. Cut into large or
small bars while still warm and
cool in the pan on a rack.

BLUEBERRY BARS

Bar Cookies

YIELD: *1 to 2 dozen*
TOTAL TIME: *1 hour and 10 minutes*

CRUST
1 cup all-purpose flour
1¼ teaspoons baking powder
½ cup vegetable shortening
¾ cup granulated sugar
1 large egg
¾ teaspoon almond extract
⅓ cup milk
1½ cups fresh blueberries, cleaned

TOPPING
2 large eggs
8 ounces cream cheese, at room
   temperature
⅓ cup powdered sugar
1 teaspoon almond extract

1 Preheat the oven to 350
degrees. Lightly grease a 9-inch
square baking pan.

2 To make the crust, combine the
flour and baking powder.

3 In a large bowl, cream the vegetable shortening and sugar. Beat
in the egg and almond extract.
Beat in the milk. Gradually blend
in the dry ingredients.

4 Spread the mixture evenly in
the prepared baking pan.

5 Sprinkle the blueberries over
the crust in the pan.

6 To make the topping, in a
medium bowl, beat the eggs and
cream cheese until smooth. Beat
in the powdered sugar and
almond extract. Spread this mixture over the blueberries.

7 Bake for 55 to 60 minutes, or
until firm to the touch. Cool in
the pan on a wire rack before cutting into large or small bars.

Brandy Alexander Brownies

Bar Cookies
Yield: 2 to 3 dozen
Total time: 35 minutes

⅔ cup all-purpose flour
1 tablespoon unsweetened cocoa
   powder
½ teaspoon baking powder
¼ teaspoon salt
½ cup vegetable shortening
¾ cup granulated sugar
2 large eggs
2 tablespoons crème de cacao
2 tablespoons brandy

1 Preheat the oven to 350 degrees. Grease a 9-inch square baking pan.

2 Combine the flour, cocoa powder, baking powder, and salt.

3 In a large bowl, cream the vegetable shortening and sugar. Beat in the eggs. Beat in the crème de cacao and brandy. Gradually blend in the dry ingredients.

4 Spread the dough evenly in the prepared baking pan.

5 Bake for 20 to 25 minutes, until the top is lightly colored. Cool in the pan on a wire rack before cutting into large or small bars.

Brazil-Nut Bars

Bar Cookies
Yield: 1 to 2 dozen
Total time: 40 minutes

Crust
½ cup vegetable shortening
1 cup all-purpose flour
¼ teaspoon salt

Topping
2 large eggs
¾ cup packed light brown sugar
1½ cups brazil nuts, ground fine
¼ teaspoon salt
½ cup flaked coconut
1 teaspoon vanilla extract
2 tablespoons all-purpose flour
Frosting to decorate

1 Preheat the oven to 375 degrees. Lightly grease a 9-inch square baking pan.

2 To make the crust, cream the vegetable shortening in a large bowl. Blend in the flour and salt.

3 Press the mixture evenly into the bottom of the prepared baking pan. Bake for 15 minutes.

4 Meanwhile make the topping: In a large bowl, beat the eggs and brown sugar together until thick. Beat in the brazil nuts and salt. Beat in the coconut, vanilla extract, and flour.

5 Spread this mixture evenly over the warm crust. Bake for 15 minutes longer, until firm to the touch.

6 Cool in the pan on a rack and top with frosting before cutting into large or small bars. (See Pantry).

Brown-and-White Brownies

Bar Cookies

YIELD: *2 to 3 dozen*
TOTAL TIME: *30 minutes*

1 tablespoon vegetable shortening
¼ cup granulated sugar
1 large egg
¾ cup milk
½ teaspoon vanilla extract
2 cups packaged cookie mix
⅓ cup chocolate syrup
1 cup (6 ounces) white chocolate chips
½ cup (3 ounces) semisweet chocolate chips

1 Preheat the oven to 375 degrees. Lightly grease a 9-inch square baking pan.

2 In a large bowl, cream the vegetable shortening and sugar. Beat in the egg. Beat in the milk and vanilla extract. Gradually blend in the cookie mix. Transfer half the batter to another bowl.

3 For the brown layer, beat the chocolate syrup into half the batter. Stir in the white chocolate chips. Spread this mixture evenly in the prepared baking pan.

4 For the white layer, stir the semisweet chocolate chips into the remaining batter. Spread evenly over the dark layer.

5 Bake for 12 to 15 minutes, or until a toothpick inserted into the center comes out clean. Cool in the pan on a wire rack before cutting into large or small bars.

Brownies I

Bar Cookies

YIELD: *1 to 2 dozen*
TOTAL TIME: *50 minutes*

4 ounces unsweetened chocolate, chopped
¾ cup vegetable shortening
2 cups granulated sugar
1 teaspoon vanilla extract
3 large eggs
1 cup all-purpose flour
1 cup walnuts, chopped fine

1 Preheat the oven to 350 degrees. Lightly grease a 13 by 9-inch baking pan.

2 In a large saucepan, melt the unsweetened chocolate and vegetable shortening over low heat, stirring until smooth. Remove from the heat and beat in the sugar and vanilla extract. Beat in the eggs. Gradually blend in the flour. Fold in the walnuts. Spread the batter evenly in the prepared baking pan.

3 Bake for 35 to 40 minutes, until a toothpick inserted into the center comes out clean. Cool in the pan on a wire rack before cutting into large or small bars.

Brownies II

Bar Cookies

YIELD: *1 to 2 dozen*
TOTAL TIME: *35 minutes*

½ cup all-purpose flour
½ teaspoon salt
¼ cup vegetable shortening
2 ounces semisweet chocolate, chopped
1 cup granulated sugar
1 teaspoon vanilla extract
2 large eggs
1 cup raisins (optional)
1 cup miniature marshmallows (optional)

1 Preheat the oven to 325 degrees. Lightly grease an 8-inch square baking pan.

2 Combine the flour and salt.

3 In a double boiler, melt the vegetable shortening and chocolate over low heat, stirring until smooth. Remove from the heat and beat in the sugar and vanilla extract. Beat in the eggs. Gradually blend in the dry ingredients. Fold in the optional raisins and marshmallows. Spread the batter evenly in the prepared baking pan.

4 Bake for 20 to 25 minutes, until a toothpick inserted in the center comes out clean. Cut into large or small squares while still warm and cool in the pan on a wire rack.

Brownies III

Bar Cookies

YIELD: *1 to 2 dozen*
TOTAL TIME: *35 minutes*

2 large eggs
1 cup granulated sugar
½ cup vegetable shortening
2 ounces bittersweet chocolate, chopped
½ cup semisweet chocolate chips
½ teaspoon vanilla extract
1 cup all-purpose flour
½ cup almonds, chopped
1 cup miniature marshmallows

1 Preheat the oven to 350 degrees. Lightly grease a 9-inch square baking pan.

2 In a medium bowl, beat the eggs until thick and light-colored. Beat in the sugar.

3 Melt the vegetable shortening, bittersweet chocolate, semisweet chocolate, and vanilla extract in the top of a double boiler over low heat, stirring until smooth. Remove from the heat and add the egg mixture in a thin steady stream, beating constantly. Gradually blend in the flour. Fold in the almonds and marshmallows. Spread the batter evenly in the prepared baking pan.

4 Bake for 25 to 30 minutes, until a toothpick inserted in the center comes out clean. Cut into large or small squares while still warm and cool in the pan on a wire rack.

Baking notes: For variation, substitute white chocolate chips for the marshmallows. If desired, frost the cooled brownies with an icing of your choice (see Icings and Frostings, in Pantry).

Brownies IV

Bar Cookies

Yield: *1 to 2 dozen*
Total time: *35 minutes*

1 cup granulated sugar
1 cup vegetable shortening
4 large eggs
1 cup chocolate syrup
1 cup all-purpose flour

Topping
⅓ cup milk
½ cup semisweet chocolate chips
½ cup walnuts, chopped

1 Preheat the oven to 350 degrees.

2 In a large bowl, cream the granulated sugar and vegetable shortening. Beat in the eggs and chocolate syrup. Gradually blend in the flour.

3 Spread the batter evenly in an ungreased 9-inch square baking pan. Bake for 25 to 30 minutes, until a toothpick inserted in the center comes out clean.

4 Meanwhile, prepare the topping: In a saucepan, bring the milk to a boil, and boil for 1 minute. Remove from the heat and add the chocolate chips and walnuts. Let cool.

5 Spread the topping over the brownies. Cool in the pan on a wire rack before cutting into large or small bars.

Baking notes: Shredded coconut can be sprinkled over the still-warm topping.

Brownies V

Bar Cookies

Yield: *1 to 2 dozen*
Total time: *50 minutes*

½ cup vegetable shortening
1 cup granulated sugar
4 large eggs
1 cup chocolate syrup
Pinch of salt
1 cup all-purpose flour
1 cup walnuts, chopped
1 cup miniature marshmallows (optional)

1 Preheat the oven to 350 degrees.

2 In a large bowl, cream the vegetable shortening and sugar. Beat in the eggs one at a time. Beat in the chocolate syrup. Beat in the salt. Gradually blend in the flour. Fold in the walnuts and the optional marshmallows. Spread the mixture evenly in an ungreased 9-inch square baking pan.

3 Bake for 35 to 40 minutes, until a toothpick inserted in the center comes out clean. Cool in the pan on a wire rack before cutting into large or small bars.

BROWNIES VI

Bar Cookies

YIELD: *1 to 2 dozen*
TOTAL TIME: *40 minutes*

¾ cup all-purpose flour
½ teaspoon baking powder
½ teaspoon salt
2 ounces unsweetened chocolate, chopped
⅓ cup unsalted butter
1 cup granulated sugar
1 teaspoon vanilla extract
2 large eggs
½ cup walnuts, chopped

1 Preheat the oven to 350 degrees. Lightly grease a 9-inch square baking pan.

2 Combine the flour, baking powder, and salt.

3 In a large saucepan, melt the chocolate and butter over low heat, stirring until smooth. Remove from the heat and beat in the sugar and vanilla extract. Beat in the eggs. Gradually blend in the dry ingredients. Stir in the walnuts. Spread the batter evenly in the prepared baking pan.

4 Bake for 30 to 35 minutes, until a toothpick inserted in the center comes out clean. Cool in the pan on a wire rack before cutting into large or small bars.

BROWNIES VII

Bar Cookies

YIELD: *1 to 2 dozen*
TOTAL TIME: *40 minutes*

½ cup vegetable shortening
¼ cup unsweetened cocoa powder
1 teaspoon vanilla extract (optional)
4 large eggs
1 cup packed light brown sugar
1 cup all-purpose flour
1 cup miniature marshmallows
½ cup walnuts, chopped

1 Preheat the oven to 350 degrees. Lightly grease a 9-inch square baking pan.

2 Melt the vegetable shortening in a medium saucepan. Stir in the cocoa powder and vanilla extract until well blended. Remove from the heat.

3 In a large bowl, beat the eggs and brown sugar until thick and light-colored. Beat in the chocolate mixture in a steady stream. Gradually blend in the flour. Fold in the marshmallows and walnuts. Spread the batter evenly in the prepared baking pan.

4 Bake for 25 to 30 minutes, until a toothpick inserted in the center comes out clean. Cool in the pan on a wire rack before cutting into large or small bars.

Brownies VIII

Bar Cookies
Yield: *1 to 2 dozen*
Total time: *30 minutes*

¼ cup unbleached flour
¼ cup soy flour
½ cup walnuts, ground fine
2 tablespoons unsweetened cocoa powder
½ teaspoon salt
1 large egg, separated
½ cup canola oil
1 cup packed light brown sugar

1 Preheat the oven to 350 degrees. Lightly grease a 9-inch square baking pan.

2 Combine the two flours, the walnuts, the cocoa powder, and salt.

3 In a small bowl, beat the egg white until stiff but not dry.

4 In a large bowl, beat the canola oil and brown sugar together. Beat in the egg yolk. Gradually blend in the dry ingredients. Fold in the beaten egg white. Spread the mixture evenly in the prepared baking pan.

5 Bake for 18 to 20 minutes, until firm to the touch. Cool in the pan on a wire rack before cutting into large or small bars.

Brownies (Sugarless)

Bar Cookies
Yield: *1 to 2 dozen*
Total time: *30 minutes*

2 ounces unsweetened chocolate, chopped
¾ cup all-purpose flour
1 teaspoon baking powder
½ cup unsalted butter, at room temperature
3 tablespoons nonnutritive sweetener (see Baking notes)
2 large eggs
½ teaspoon vanilla extract
½ cup walnuts, chopped fine

1 Preheat the oven to 350 degrees. Lightly grease an 8-inch square baking pan.

2 Melt the chocolate in a double boiler over low heat, stirring until smooth. Remove from the heat.

3 Combine the flour and baking powder.

4 In a large bowl, cream the butter and sweetener. Beat in the melted chocolate. Beat in the eggs and vanilla. Gradually blend in the dry ingredients. Fold in the walnuts. Spread the batter evenly in the prepared baking pan.

5 Bake for 25 to 30 minutes, until firm to the touch. Cool in the pan on a wire rack before cutting into large or small squares.

Baking notes: Although created for diabetics, these brownies will appeal to anyone on a sugar-restricted diet. There are several nonnutritive sweeteners on the market.

Brown Sugar Cocoa Brownies

Bar Cookies

YIELD: *1 to 2 dozen*
TOTAL TIME: *30 minutes*

½ cup all-purpose flour
1 teaspoon baking powder
½ cup unsweetened cocoa powder
¼ teaspoon salt
3 large eggs
1¼ cups packed light brown sugar
1 teaspoon vanilla extract
1 cup walnuts, chopped fine

1 Preheat the oven to 325 degrees. Lightly grease a 9-inch square baking pan.

2 Combine the flour, baking powder, cocoa powder, and salt.

3 In a large bowl, beat the eggs and brown sugar. Beat in the vanilla extract until thick. Gradually blend in the dry ingredients. Fold in the walnuts. Spread this mixture evenly in the prepared baking pan.

4 Bake for 20 to 25 minutes, until a toothpick inserted in the center comes out clean. Cut into large or small bars and cool in the pan on a wire rack.

Buttermilk Brownies

Bar Cookies

YIELD: *1 to 2 dozen*
TOTAL TIME: *30 minutes*

2 cups all-purpose flour
1¾ cups granulated sugar
¼ cup packed light brown sugar
½ teaspoon salt
1 cup vegetable shortening
⅓ cup unsweetened cocoa powder
1 cup water
1 teaspoon baking soda
1 tablespoon warm water
2 large eggs
½ cup buttermilk
1 teaspoon vanilla extract

1 Preheat the oven to 375 degrees. Lightly grease a 13 by 9-inch baking pan.

2 Combine the flour, both sugars, and salt.

3 In a large saucepan, combine the vegetable shortening, cocoa powder, and the 1 cup water, stir until smooth and bring to a boil over high heat. Remove from the heat.

4 Dissolve the baking soda in the warm water and beat into the cocoa mixture. Beat in the eggs. Beat in the buttermilk and vanilla extract. Gradually blend in the dry ingredients. Pour the batter into the prepared baking pan.

5 Bake for 18 to 20 minutes, or until a toothpick inserted in the center comes out clean. Cool in the pan on a wire rack before cutting into large or small bars.

Butterscotch Bars

Bar Cookies

YIELD: *2 to 3 dozen*
TOTAL TIME: *40 minutes*

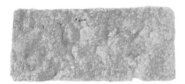

2 cups all-purpose flour
2 teaspoons baking powder
½ cup vegetable shortening
2 cups packed light brown sugar
2 large eggs
1 teaspoon vanilla extract
1 cup shredded coconut
1 cup walnuts, chopped

1 Preheat the oven to 350 degrees. Lightly grease a 13 by 9-inch baking pan.

2 Combine the flour and baking powder.

3 In a large bowl, cream the vegetable shortening and brown sugar. Beat in the eggs. Beat in the vanilla extract. Gradually blend in the dry ingredients. Fold in the coconut and walnuts. Spread the mixture evenly in the prepared baking pan.

4 Bake for 20 to 25 minutes, until a toothpick inserted into the center comes out clean. Cut into large or small bars and cool in the pan on a wire rack.

Butterscotch Brownies I

Bar Cookies

YIELD: *1 to 2 dozen*
TOTAL TIME: *35 minutes*

⅔ cup all-purpose flour
½ cup walnuts, ground fine
1 teaspoon baking powder
¼ teaspoon salt
¼ cup vegetable shortening
1 cup packed light brown sugar
1 large egg
1 teaspoon vanilla extract

1 Preheat the oven to 350 degrees. Lightly grease an 8-inch square baking pan.

2 Combine the flour, walnuts, baking powder, and salt.

3 In a large bowl, cream the vegetable shortening and sugar. Beat in the egg. Beat in the vanilla extract. Gradually blend in the dry ingredients. Spread the dough evenly in the prepared baking pan.

4 Bake for 20 to 25 minutes, or until a toothpick inserted in the center comes out clean. Cut into large or small bars and cool in the pan on a wire rack.

BUTTERSCOTCH BROWNIES II

Bar Cookies

YIELD: *2 to 3 dozen*
TOTAL TIME: *45 minutes*

1½ cups all-purpose flour
2 teaspoons baking powder
¼ teaspoon salt
⅔ cup vegetable shortening
2 cups packed light brown sugar
2 large eggs
1 teaspoon almond extract
1 cup almonds, chopped
¼ cup sliced almonds

1 Preheat the oven to 350 degrees. Lightly grease a 9-inch square baking pan.

2 Combine the flour, baking powder, and salt.

3 In a large bowl, cream the vegetable shortening and brown sugar. Beat in the eggs. Beat in the almond extract. Gradually blend in the dry ingredients. Stir in the chopped almonds.

4 Spread the batter evenly in the prepared baking pan. Sprinkle the sliced almonds over the top and press down lightly.

5 Bake for 30 to 35 minutes, until firm and a toothpick inserted in the center comes out clean. Cool in the pan on a wire rack before cutting into large or small bars.

BUTTERSCOTCH BROWNIES III

Bar Cookies

YIELD: *1 to 2 dozen*
TOTAL TIME: *30 minutes*

1½ cups all-purpose flour
1 teaspoon baking powder
½ teaspoon salt
⅔ cup butter, at room temperature
⅔ cups packed dark brown sugar
⅔ cup dark corn syrup
2 large eggs
1 teaspoon hazelnut extract
1 cup hazelnuts, chopped

1 Preheat the oven to 325 degrees. Lightly grease a 9-inch square baking pan.

2 Combine the flour, baking powder, and salt.

3 In a large bowl, cream the butter and brown sugar. Beat in the corn syrup. Beat in the eggs and hazelnut extract. Gradually blend in the dry ingredients. Stir in the hazelnuts. Scrape the mixture into the prepared baking pan.

4 Bake for 20 to 25 minutes, until firm to the touch. Cool in the pan on a wire rack before cutting into large or small bars.

BUTTERSCOTCH CHEESECAKE BARS

Bar Cookies

YIELD: *1 to 2 dozen*
TOTAL TIME: *30 minutes*

BUTTERSCOTCH CHEWS

Bar Cookies

YIELD: *1 to 2 dozen*
TOTAL TIME: *35 minutes*

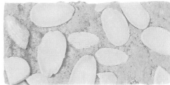

CRUST
¾ cup butterscotch chips
⅓ cup butter, at room temperature
2 cups graham cracker crumbs
1 cup walnuts, ground fine

FILLING
8 ounces cream cheese, at room temperature
One 14-ounce can sweetened condensed milk
1 large egg
1 teaspoon vanilla extract

1 Preheat the oven to 350 degrees. Lightly grease a 13 by 9-inch baking pan.

2 To make the crust, melt the butterscotch chips and butter in a medium saucepan, stirring until smooth. Remove from the heat and blend in the graham cracker crumbs and walnuts. Spread half of this mixture evenly into the bottom of the prepared baking pan.

3 To make the filling, beat the cream cheese and condensed milk together in a small bowl. Beat in the egg and vanilla extract. Pour this mixture over the crust.

4 Spread the remaining crust mixture over the filling.

5 Bake for 25 to 30 minutes, until a knife inserted into the center comes out clean. Cool in the pan on a wire rack before cutting into large or small bars.

2 cups all-purpose flour
2 teaspoons baking powder
¼ teaspoon salt
½ cup vegetable shortening
2 cups packed light brown sugar
2 large eggs
½ teaspoon vanilla extract
1⅓ cups sliced almonds

1 Preheat the oven to 350 degrees. Lightly grease a 9-inch square baking pan.

2 Combine the flour, baking powder, and salt.

3 In a large bowl, cream the vegetable shortening and sugar. Beat in the eggs. Beat in the vanilla extract. Gradually blend in the dry ingredients.

4 Spread the mixture evenly in the prepared baking pan. Sprinkle the almonds over the top and press down gently.

5 Bake for 20 to 25 minutes, until firm to the touch. Cool in the pan on a wire rack before cutting into large or small bars.

BUTTERSCOTCH SHORTBREAD

Bar Cookies

YIELD: *1 to 2 dozen*
TOTAL TIME: *30 minutes*

1/2 cup butter, at room temperature
½ cup packed light brown sugar
1 large egg
2 cups all-purpose flour

1 Preheat the oven to 350 degrees.

2 In a large bowl, cream the butter and brown sugar. Beat in the egg. Gradually blend in the flour.

3 Spread the dough evenly in an ungreased 9-inch square baking pan. Score the bars, using with the back of a knife.

4 Bake for 15 to 20 minutes, until firm to the touch. Cut into bars and cool in the pan on a rack.

BUTTERSCOTCH SQUARES

Bar Cookies

YIELD: *1 to 2 dozen*
TOTAL TIME: *40 minutes*

1¼ cups all-purpose flour
1 teaspoon baking powder
¼ teaspoon salt
½ cup vegetable shortening
½ cup peanut butter
1½ cups packed light brown sugar
2 large eggs
1 teaspoon vanilla extract

1 Preheat the oven to 350 degrees. Lightly grease a 9-inch square baking pan.

2 Combine the flour, baking powder, and salt.

3 In medium saucepan, combine the vegetable shortening, peanut butter, and brown sugar and heat over medium heat, stirring, until the shortening melts and the sugar dissolves. Remove from the heat and let cool slightly.

4 Beat the eggs into the peanut butter mixture. Beat in the vanilla extract. Gradually blend in the dry ingredients.

5 Spread the mixture evenly in the prepared baking pan.

6 Bake for 25 to 30 minutes, or until a toothpick inserted in the center comes out clean. Cool in the pan on a wire rack before cutting into large or small bars.

CARAMEL SUGAR SQUARES

Bar Cookies

YIELD: *2 to 3 dozen*

TOTAL TIME: *45 minutes*

CARAMEL
½ cup granulated sugar
½ cup boiling water

COOKIES
2¼ cups all-purpose flour
2 teaspoons baking powder
¼ teaspoon salt
½ cup vegetable shortening
1¼ cups granulated sugar
2 large eggs
1 teaspoon vanilla extract
½ cup walnuts, chopped

TOPPING
1 tablespoon butter or margarine, at
   room temperature
1 cup powdered sugar
About 1 tablespoon milk

1 Preheat the oven to 375 degrees. Lightly grease a 13 by 9-inch baking pan.

2 To make the caramel, put the sugar in a heavy saucepan and cook over low heat, stirring constantly, until the sugar melts. Continue cooking, without stirring, until a golden brown caramel. Immediately remove from the heat and slowly stir in the boiling water. Return to low heat and stir until any lumps of caramel have dissolved. Bring to a boil, and boil until reduced to ⅓ cup. Set aside.

4 In a large saucepan, melt the vegetable shortening. Beat in the sugar. Remove from the heat and beat in the eggs one at a time. Beat in the vanilla extract. Beat in 3 tablespoons of the caramel. Gradually blend in the dry ingredients. Fold in the walnuts.

5 Spread the mixture evenly in the prepared baking pan. Bake for 15 to 18 minutes, or until the top is golden-colored.

6 Meanwhile, make the topping: In a medium bowl, cream the butter and powdered sugar. Beat in the remaining caramel. Beat in just enough enough milk to make the mixture spreadable.

7 Spread the topping over the warm cookies. Cool in the pan on a wire rack before cutting into large or small bars.

Caramel Bars

Bar Cookies

Yield: *1 to 2 dozen*
Total time: *45 minutes*

One 14-ounce package caramels (light or dark)
⅔ cup evaporated milk
¾ cup vegetable shortening.
1 package German chocolate cake mix
1 cup peanuts, chopped
1 cup (6 ounces) semisweet chocolate chips

1 Preheat the oven to 350 degrees. Lightly grease a 9-inch square baking pan.

2 In the top of a double boiler, melt the caramel candy with ⅓ cup of the evaporated milk, stirring until smooth. Remove from the heat.

3 In a large bowl, combine the vegetable shortening and cake mix and beat until smooth. Beat in the milk and stir in the peanuts. The mixture will be crumbly.

4 Press half of the cake mixture into the prepared baking pan. Bake for 8 minutes.

5 Sprinkle the chocolate chips over the warm dough. Spread the caramel mixture over the chocolate chips and spread the remaining cake mixture over the caramel layer.

6 Bake for 18 to 20 minutes longer, until firm to the touch. Cool in the pan on a wire rack before cutting into large or small bars.

Carrot Coconut Bars

Bar Cookies

Yield: *1 to 3 dozen*
Total time: *45 minutes*

1¼ cups all-purpose flour
1 teaspoon baking powder
1 teaspoon ground cardamom
¼ teaspoon ground nutmeg
¼ teaspoon salt
½ cup vegetable shortening
1 cup granulated sugar
2 large eggs
¾ cup grated carrots
2 tablespoons Amaretto
1 tablespoon orange liqueur
¾ cup shredded coconut
¾ cup almonds, chopped

1 Preheat the oven to 375 degrees. Grease a 13 by 9-inch baking pan.

2 Combine the flour, baking powder, spices, and salt.

3 In a large bowl, cream the vegetable shortening and sugar. Beat in the eggs. Beat in the carrots. Beat in the Amaretto and orange liqueur. Gradually blend in the dry ingredients. Fold in the coconut and almonds. Spread the batter evenly in the prepared baking pan.

4 Bake for 20 to 25 minutes, until golden brown on top. Cool in the pan on a wire rack before cutting into large or small bars.

CASHEW BARS

Bar Cookies

YIELD: *2 to 3 dozen*
TOTAL TIME: *30 minutes*

2 cups all-purpose flour
1 cup cashews, ground fine
2 teaspoons baking powder
1 teaspoon baking soda
1 teaspoon ground nutmeg
½ cup vegetable shortening
3 large eggs
½ cup mashed bananas
½ cup cashews, chopped

1 Preheat the oven to 350 degrees. Lightly grease a 13 by 9-inch baking pan.

2 Combine the flour, ground cashews, baking powder, baking soda, and nutmeg.

3 In a large bowl, beat the vegetable shortening and eggs together. Beat in the bananas. Gradually blend in the dry ingredients.

4 Spread the mixture evenly in the prepared baking pan. Sprinkle the chopped cashews over the batter and press down gently.

5 Bake for 18 to 20 minutes, or until a toothpick inserted in the center comes out clean. Cool in the pan on a wire rack before cutting into large or small bars.

CASHEW-CARAMEL COOKIES

Bar Cookies

YIELD: *1 to 2 dozen*
TOTAL TIME: *35 minutes*

¾ cup all-purpose flour
½ teaspoon baking powder
¼ teaspoon salt
2 large eggs
½ cup granulated sugar
2 tablespoons light brown sugar
½ cup cashews, chopped

TOPPING
2 tablespoons butter
1 tablespoon evaporated milk
2 tablespoons light brown sugar
½ cup cashews, chopped

1 Preheat the oven to 350 degrees. Lightly grease a 9-inch square baking pan.

2 Combine the flour, baking powder, and salt.

3 In a large bowl, beat the eggs, and both sugars together until thick. Add the cashews. Gradually blend in the dry ingredients.

4 Spread the dough evenly in the prepared baking pan. Bake for 25 minutes.

5 Meanwhile, make the topping in a saucepan: Combine all the ingredients and cook, stirring, until smooth. Remove from the heat.

6 Preheat the boiler.

7 Spread the topping over the warm cookies and place under the broiler for 1 minute, or until the topping starts to bubble. Cut into large or small bars while still warm, and cool in the pan on a rack.

CASHEW GRANOLA BARS

Bar Cookies

YIELD: *3 to 4 dozen*
TOTAL TIME: *45 minutes*

6 cups rolled oats
1 cup shredded coconuts
1 cup wheat germ
1 cup golden raisins
½ cup sunflower seeds, shelled
¼ cup sesame seeds, toasted
1 teaspoon ground allspice
1 cup honey
¾ cup canola oil
⅓ cup water
1½ teaspoons vanilla extract

1 Preheat the oven to 350 degrees. Lightly grease a 13 by 9-inch baking pan.

2 In a large bowl, combine the oats, coconut, wheat germ, raisins, sunflower seeds, sesame seeds, and allspice.

3 In a medium saucepan, combine the honey, oil, water, and vanilla extract and heat until warm.

4 Pour over the dry ingredients and blend thoroughly. Spread the mixture evenly in the prepared baking pan.

5 Bake for 30 to 40 minutes, until firm and no longer sticking. Cut into large or small bars while still warm, and cool in the pan on a wire rack.

CHEESECAKE COOKIES

Bar Cookies

YIELD: *1 to 3 dozen*
TOTAL TIME: *40 minutes*

CRUST
½ cup canola oil
¼ cup powdered sugar
24 gingersnaps, crushed

FILLING
1 pound cream cheese, at room temperature
½ cup granulated sugar
2 large eggs
1 tablespoon fresh lemon juice
1 tablespoon marsala
1 tablespoon honey
¼ teaspoon ground allspice

1 Preheat the oven to 375 degrees.

2 To make the crust, beat the canola oil and powdered sugar together in a large bowl. Gradually work in the crushed gingersnaps.

3 Press the mixture evenly into an ungreased 9-inch square baking pan.

4 Bake for about 6 minutes.

5 Meanwhile, make the filling: In a large bowl, beat the cream cheese and sugar until creamy. Beat in the eggs. Beat in the lemon juice, marsala, honey, and allspice.

6 Spread the filling over the hot crust. Bake for 12 to 15 minutes longer, until set. Cool in the pan on a wire rack before cutting into large or small bars.

Baking notes: For dessert, serve cut into large bars with sliced strawberries and whipped cream.

CHERRY-ALMOND SQUARES

Bar Cookies

YIELD: *1 to 2 dozen*
TOTAL TIME: *45 minutes*

CRUST
1 cup all-purpose flour
¼ teaspoon salt
½ cup vegetable shortening
⅓ cup powdered sugar

TOPPING
3 ounces cream cheese
½ cup crumbled almond paste
1 large egg
½ cup red maraschino cherries, chopped

1 Preheat the oven to 350 degrees.

2 Combine the flour and salt.

3 To make the crust, cream the vegetable shortening and powdered sugar in a large bowl,. Gradually blend in the dry ingredients. The mixture will be crumbly.

4 Press the mixture evenly into the bottom of an ungreased 9-inch square baking pan. Bake for 15 minutes.

5 Meanwhile, make the topping: In a large bowl, beat the cream cheese and almond paste until smooth and creamy. Beat in the egg. Fold in the maraschino cherries.

6 Spread the topping over the warm crust. Bake for 15 minutes longer, until set. Cool in the pan on a wire rack before cutting into large or small bars.

CHERRY SQUARES

Bar Cookies

YIELD: *2 to 3 dozen*
TOTAL TIME: *45 minutes*

2 cups all-purpose flour
¼ teaspoon salt
¾ cup vegetable shortening
1 cup granulated sugar
1 large egg
1 teaspoon vanilla extract
1½ cups shredded coconut
One 10-ounce jar cherry preserves

1 Preheat the oven to 350 degrees. Lightly grease a 13 by 9-inch baking pan.

2 Combine the flour and salt.

3 In a large bowl, cream the vegetable shortening and sugar. Beat in the egg. Beat in the vanilla extract. Gradually blend in the dry ingredients. Fold in the coconut.

4 Press three-quarters of the dough evenly into the prepared baking pan. Spread the cherry preserves over the dough. Crumble the remaining dough over the preserves.

5 Bake for 25 to 30 minutes, until firm and lightly colored on top. Cool in the pan on a wire rack before cutting into large or small bars.

CHERRY STRIPS

Bar Cookies

YIELD: *3 to 5 dozen*
TOTAL TIME: *35 minutes*
CHILLING TIME: *2 hours*

CRUST
2 cups all-purpose flour
¼ cup granulated sugar
1½ tablespoons grated lemon zest
¾ cup vegetable shortening
3 tablespoons sour cream
½ teaspoon almond extract

FILLING
**1½ cups canned cherries, pitted &
    sliced**
1 tablespoon raisins
¼ cup granulated sugar
1 large egg yolk, beaten
Powdered sugar for dusting

1 To make the crust, combine the flour, sugar, and lemon zest in a large bowl. Cut in the vegetable shortening. Stir in the sour cream and almond extract.

2 Divide the dough in half. Wrap in waxed paper and set aside at room temperature for 2 hours.

3 Drain the cherries and reserve for at least one hour.

4 Preheat the oven to 325 degrees. Lightly grease a 9-inch square baking pan.

5 On a floured surface, roll out half the dough to a 9-inch square. Fit it into the prepared baking pan. Layer the sliced cherries over the dough. Sprinkle the raisins and then the sugar over the top.

6 Roll out the remaining dough to a 9-inch square. Cut into 1-inch strips. Arrange the strips over filling in a lattice pattern. Brush the strips with the egg yolk.

7 Bake for 18 to 20 minutes, until the lattice strips start to color. Dust the top with powdered sugar and cool in the pan on a wire rack before cutting into large or small strips.

Baking notes: Shredded coconut is a good addition to these bars. The cherries may be sliced, diced, or crushed.

Chewy Pecan Bars

Bar Cookies

Yield: *1 to 2 dozen*
Total time: *60 minutes*

1 cup all-purpose flour
½ teaspoon baking powder
1 tablespoon ground cinnamon
¼ teaspoon salt
1 cup vegetable shortening
1 cup granulated sugar
2 large egg yolks

Topping
2 large egg whites
1½ teaspoons powdered sugar
1 cup pecans, chopped

1 Preheat the oven to 300 degrees.

2 Combine the flour, baking powder, cinnamon, and salt.

3 In a large bowl, cream the vegetable shortening and sugar. Beat in the large egg yolks. Gradually blend in the dry ingredients. Spread the dough evenly into a 13 by 9-inch square baking pan.

4 To make the topping, beat the large egg whites in a medium bowl, until stiff and frothy. Fold in the powdered sugar. Spread the topping over the dough. Sprinkle the chopped pecans over the top.

5 Bake for 40 to 45 minutes, or until the topping is lightly colored. Cool in the pan on a wire rack before cutting into large or small bars.

Chocolate Chews

Bar Cookies

Yield: *2 to 3 dozen*
Total time: *50 minutes*

½ cup vegetable shortening
2 ounces bittersweet chocolate, chopped
2 large eggs
1 cup granulated sugar
½ teaspoon almond extract
½ cup all-purpose flour
1 cup slivered almonds

1 Preheat the oven to 350 degrees. Lightly grease an 11 by 7-inch baking pan.

2 Melt the vegetable shortening and chocolate in a double boiler over low heat, stirring until smooth. Remove from the heat and beat in the eggs one at a time, beating thoroughly after each addition. Beat in the sugar and almond extract. Blend in the flour.

3 Spread the dough evenly in the prepared baking pan. Sprinkle the slivered almonds over the top

4 Bake for 35 to 40 minutes, until firm to the touch. Cool in the pan on a wire rack before cutting into large or small bars.

CHOCOLATE CHIP BAR COOKIES

Bar Cookies
YIELD: *2 to 3 dozen*
TOTAL TIME: *45 minutes*

2 cups all-purpose flour
1 teaspoon baking powder
¼ teaspoon baking soda
¼ teaspoon salt
1 cup vegetable shortening
1½ cups packed light brown sugar
2 large eggs
2 tablespoons milk
1 teaspoon vanilla extract
1 cup (6 ounces) semisweet choco-
    late chips

1 Preheat the oven to 350 degrees. Lightly grease a 9-inch square baking pan.

2 Combine the flour, baking powder, baking soda, and salt.

3 In a large bowl, cream the vegetable shortening and brown sugar. Beat in the eggs. Beat in the milk and vanilla extract. Gradually blend in the dry ingredients. Fold in the chocolate chips.

4 Spread the dough evenly in the prepared baking pan.

5 Bake for 25 to 30 minutes, or until golden brown on top. Cool in the pan on a wire rack before cutting into large or small bars.

Baking notes: For an unusual variation, substitute white crème de menthe for the vanilla extract.

CHOCOLATE CHIP BARS

Bar Cookies
YIELD: *3 to 4 dozen*
TOTAL TIME: *45 minutes*

1¼ cups whole wheat flour
1 teaspoon baking powder
⅓ cup unsalted butter, at room
    temperature
1¼ cups raw sugar
2 large eggs
½ cup walnuts, chopped fine
½ cup semisweet chocolate chips

1 Preheat the oven to 350 degrees. Lightly grease a 9-inch square baking pan.

2 Combine the flour and baking powder.

3 In a large bowl, cream the butter and raw sugar. Beat in the eggs. Gradually blend in the dry ingredients. Fold in the walnuts and chocolate chips. Press the dough evenly into the prepared baking pan.

4 Bake for 18 to 20 minutes, or until golden brown on top. Cool in the pan on a wire rack before cutting into large or small bars.

Baking notes: These can be baked in a 13 by 9-inch baking pan, but the texture of the cookies will be drier so bake for a shorter time.

CHOCOLATE CHIP NUT BARS

Bar Cookies
YIELD: *2 to 3 dozen*
TOTAL TIME: *45 minutes*

½ cup all-purpose flour
½ teaspoon baking powder
¼ teaspoon salt
1 large egg
½ cup granulated sugar
1 teaspoon butter, melted
2 teaspoons hot water
⅔ cup walnuts, chopped fine
½ cup almonds, chopped fine
1 cup (6 ounces) semisweet chocolate chips

1 Preheat the oven to 325 degrees. Lightly grease an 8-inch square baking pan.

2 Combine the flour, baking powder, and salt.

3 In a large bowl, beat the egg until thick and light-colored. Beat in the sugar. Beat in the butter and and hot water. Beat in the nuts. Gradually blend in the dry ingredients. Fold in the chocolate chips.

4 Spread the batter evenly into the prepared baking pan. Bake for 25 to 30 minutes, or until lightly colored on top. Cool in the pan on a wire rack before cutting into large or small bars.

CHOCOLATE CHIP SQUARES

Bar Cookies
YIELD: *3 to 5 dozen*
TOTAL TIME: *30 minutes*

CRUST
2¼ cups all-purpose flour
1 teaspoon baking soda
½ teaspoon salt
1 cup canola oil
½ cup granulated sugar
¾ cup packed light brown sugar
1 large egg
2½ teaspoons white crème de menthe
1⅓ cups (8 ounces) semisweet chocolate chips

TOPPING
½ cup (3 ounces) semisweet chocolate chips

1 Preheat the oven to 350 degrees. Lightly grease a 13 by 9-inch baking pan.

2 Combine the flour, baking soda, and salt.

3 In a large bowl, beat the canola oil and the two sugars. Beat in the egg. Beat in the crème de menthe. Gradually blend in the dry ingredients. Fold in the chocolate chips.

4 Spread the dough evenly in the prepared pan. Bake for 15 to 20 minutes, until the top is golden brown.

5 For the topping, spread the chocolate chips over the hot cookies. With a spatula, spread the melted chocolate chips evenly over the top. Cool in the pan on a wire rack before cutting into large or small bars.

CHOCOLATE-COCONUT TEA STRIPS

Bar Cookies

YIELD: *3 to 4 dozen*
TOTAL TIME: *35 minutes*

1½ cups all-purpose flour
1½ teaspoons baking powder
¼ teaspoon salt
6 tablespoons butter, at room
   temperature
¾ cup plus 2 tablespoons granulated
   sugar
1 large egg
2 tablespoons milk
½ teaspoon vanilla extract
1 ounce bittersweet chocolate,
   chopped
1 teaspoon grated orange zest
¼ cup pecans, chopped
⅔ cup shredded coconut

1 Preheat the oven to 375 degrees. Lightly grease two 8-inch square baking pans.

2 Combine the flour, baking powder, and salt.

3 In a large bowl, cream the butter and sugar. Beat in the egg. Beat in the milk and vanilla extract. Gradually blend in the dry ingredients. Divide the dough in half and transfer half to another bowl.

4 Melt the chocolate in a double boiler over low heat, stirring until smooth. Remove from the heat and work into half the dough.

5 On a floured surface, roll out the chocolate dough to an 8-inch square Fit it into one of the prepared baking pans and sprinkle with 1 tablespoon of the sugar and half the orange zest.

6 Bake 10 to 15 minutes, until firm to the touch. Cool in the pan on a wire rack before cutting into 2 by 1-inch strips.

7 Meanwhile, blend the pecans and coconut into the remaining dough. Roll out the dough, fit it into the second baking pan, and sprinkle with the remaining 1 tablespoon of sugar and remaining orange zest.

8 Bake as directed, cool, and cut into strips.

Chocolate-Coconut Bars

Bar Cookies

YIELD: *1 to 2 dozen*
TOTAL TIME: *40 minutes*

1½ cups crushed graham crackers
One 14-ounce can sweetened condensed milk
1½ cups flaked coconut
½ cup semisweet chocolate chips

1 Preheat the oven to 350 degrees. Grease a 9-inch square baking pan.

2 In a large bowl, combine all the ingredients, stirring until well blended. Press the mixture evenly into the prepared baking pan.

3 Bake for 30 minutes until set. Cool in the pan on a wire rack before cutting into large or small bars.

Chocolate de la Harina de Avena Brownies

Bar Cookies

YIELD: *2 to 3 dozen*
TOTAL TIME: *35 minutes*

3 ounces bittersweet chocolate, chopped
1 cup all-purpose flour
1 cup almonds, chopped fine
½ teaspoon salt
⅔ cup vegetable shortening
1 cup packed light brown sugar
½ cup granulated sugar
4 large eggs
2 teaspoons vanilla extract
1 cup rolled oats

1 Preheat the oven to 325 degrees. Lightly grease a 13 by 9-inch baking pan.

2 Melt the chocolate in a double boiler over low heat, stirring until smooth. Remove from the heat.

3 Combine the flour, almonds, and salt.

4 In a large bowl, cream the vegetable shortening and the two sugars. Beat in the eggs. Beat in the vanilla extract, then the melted chocolate. Gradually blend in the dry ingredients. Fold in the oats.

5 Spread the dough evenly in the prepared baking pan. Bake for 25 to 30 minutes, or until a toothpick inserted into the center comes out clean but not dry; do not overbake. Cool in the pan on a wire rack before cutting into large or small bars.

Baking notes: Add 1 cup of raisins to the dough if desired. These are traditional Mexican cookies.

CHOCOLATE DELIGHT BARS

Bar Cookies
YIELD: *1 to 2 dozen*
TOTAL TIME: *40 minutes*

CRUST
½ cup butter, at room temperature
3 tablespoons powdered sugar
2 large yolks
1 teaspoon instant coffee crystals
1 tablespoon warm water
2 cups all-purpose flour

TOPPING
½ cup semisweet chocolate chips
2 large egg whites
¼ cup granulated sugar
¼ cup almonds, ground fine
¼ cup almonds, chopped

1 Preheat the oven to 350 degrees. Lightly grease a 9-inch square baking pan.

2 In a large bowl, combine the butter, powdered sugar, egg yolks, coffee crystals, and water and beat until well blended. Gradually blend in the flour. The mixture will be crumbly.

3 Press the mixture evenly into the bottom of the prepared baking pan. Bake for 20 minutes.

4 Meanwhile, melt the chocolate in the top of a double boiler, stirring until smooth. Remove from the heat.

5 In a medium bowl, beat the egg whites until foamy. Gradually beat in the sugar and beat until the whites hold stiff peaks. In a steady stream, beat in the melted chocolate. Fold in the ground almonds.

6 Spread the topping over the warm crust. Sprinkle with the chopped almonds and bake for 20 minutes longer, until set.

CHOCOLATE OATMEAL BARS

Bar Cookies
YIELD: *3 to 4 dozen*
TOTAL TIME: *45 minutes*

CRUST
2½ cups all-purpose flour
1 teaspoon baking soda
1 teaspoon salt
1 cup vegetable shortening
2 cups packed light brown sugar
2 large eggs
2 teaspoons vanilla extract
3 cups rolled oats

FILLING
2 cups (12 ounces) semisweet chocolate chips
2 tablespoons butter
One 14-ounce can sweetened condensed milk
2 teaspoons vanilla extract
1 cup walnuts, chopped

1 Preheat the oven to 350 degrees.

2 To make the crust, combine the flour, baking soda, and salt.

3 In a large bowl, cream the vegetable shortening and brown sugar. Beat in the eggs and vanilla. Gradually blend in the dry ingredients. Fold in the rolled oats.

4 Press two-thirds of the crust mixture evenly into an ungreased 13 by 9-inch baking pan.

5 To prepare the filling, melt the chocolate chips and butter in a double boiler over low heat, stirring until smooth. Remove from the heat and stir in the condensed milk and vanilla extract. Fold in the nuts.

6 Spread the filling evenly over the crust in the baking pan. Press the remaining crust mixture on top of the filling.

7 Bake for 25 to 30 minutes, until firm to the touch. Cool in the pan on a wire rack before cutting into large or small bars.

CHOCOLATE PUDDING BROWNIES

Bar Cookies

YIELD: *1 to 2 dozen*
TOTAL TIME: *45 minutes*

½ cup all-purpose flour
One 4-ounce package chocolate
  pudding mix
½ teaspoon baking powder
¼ teaspoon salt
6 tablespoons vegetable shortening
⅔ cup granulated sugar
2 large eggs
¼ cup milk
1 teaspoon vanilla extract
½ cup walnuts, chopped
Powdered sugar for sprinkling

1 Preheat the oven to 350 degrees. Lightly grease a 9-inch square baking pan.

2 Combine the flour, chocolate pudding mix, baking powder, and salt.

3 In a large bowl, cream the vegetable shortening and sugar. Beat in the eggs. Beat in the milk and vanilla extract. Gradually blend in the dry ingredients. Fold in the walnuts. Spread the mixture evenly in the prepared baking pan.

4 Bake for 25 to 30 minutes, until a toothpick inserted in the center comes out clean. Cool in the pan on a wire rack.

5 Place a paper doily on top of the cooled cookies and sprinkle with powdered sugar. Remove the doily and cut into large or small bars.

CHOCOLATE SQUARES

Bar Cookies

YIELD: *1 to 3 dozen*
TOTAL TIME: *30 minutes*

2 ounces semisweet chocolate,
  chopped
1½ cups all-purpose flour
½ teaspoon baking soda
¼ teaspoon salt
½ cup vegetable shortening
1 cup packed light brown sugar
1 large egg
1 teaspoon vanilla extract
½ cup shredded coconut
½ cup walnuts, chopped

1 Preheat the oven to 350 degrees. Lightly grease a 13 by 9-inch baking pan.

2 Melt the chocolate in a double boiler over low heat, stirring until smooth. Remove from the heat.

3 Combine the flour, baking soda, and salt.

4 In a large bowl, cream the vegetable shortening and brown sugar. Beat in the egg. Beat in the melted chocolate and vanilla extract. Gradually blend in the dry ingredients.

5 Spread the batter evenly in the prepared baking pan. Sprinkle the coconut and walnuts over the top.

6 Bake for 10 to 12 minutes, until firm to the touch. Cool in the pan on a wire rack before cutting into large or small bars.

CHUNKY CHOCOLATE BROWNIES

Bar Cookies

YIELD: *1 to 2 dozen*
TOTAL TIME: *30 minutes*

½ cup plus 2 tablespoons vegetable shortening
¼ cup unsweetened cocoa powder
1 cup granulated sugar
2 large eggs
1 teaspoon vanilla extract
⅔ cup all-purpose flour
2½ ounces milk chocolate, cut into small chunks
2½ ounces white chocolate, cut into small chunks
¾ cup chocolate glaze
12 to 24 walnut halves for decoration

1 Preheat the oven to 350 degrees. Lightly grease a 9-inch square baking pan.

2 In the top of a double boiler, melt the vegetable shortening with the cocoa powder, stirring until smooth. Remove from the the eggs and vanilla extract. Gradually blend in the flour. Fold in the milk and white chocolate chunks. Spread the mixture evenly in the prepared baking pan.

3 Bake for 18 to 20 minutes until firm to the touch.

4 Spread the chocolate glaze over the top. Cut into large or small bars, then place a walnut in the center of each. Cool in the pan on a wire rack.

CITRUS BARS

Bar Cookies

YIELD: *2 to 3 dozen*
TOTAL TIME: *45 minutes*

2½ cups all-purpose flour
2 teaspoons baking powder
1 teaspoon baking soda
½ teaspoon ground cinnamon
¼ teaspoon ground cloves
¼ cup vegetable shortening
2 large eggs
1½ cups grapefruit juice
1 teaspoon orange extract
1 cup cranberries, chopped
1 cup walnuts, chopped

TOPPING
¾ cup flaked coconut
¾ cup crushed pineapple, drained

1 Preheat the oven to 350 degrees. Lightly grease a 13 by 9-inch baking pan.

2 Combine the flour, baking powder, baking soda, and spices.

3 In a large bowl, beat the vegetable shortening, eggs, grapefruit juice, and orange extract. Gradually blend in the dry ingredients. Fold in the cranberries and walnuts.

4 Spread the mixture evenly in the prepared baking pan. Sprinkle the coconut and pineapple over the top.

5 Bake for 20 to 25 minutes, until firm to the touch. Cool in the pan on a wire rack before cutting into large or small bars.

Cocoa Brownies

Bar Cookies
YIELD: *2 to 3 dozen*
TOTAL TIME: *45 minutes*

½ cup all-purpose flour
½ cup unsweetened cocoa powder
1 teaspoon baking powder
Pinch of salt
3 large eggs
1¼ cups packed light brown sugar
1 teaspoon vanilla extract
1 cup walnuts, chopped

1 Preheat the oven to 325 degrees. Lightly grease a 9-inch square baking pan.

2 Combine the flour, cocoa, baking powder, and salt.

3 In a large bowl, beat the eggs and brown sugar together until thick. Beat in the vanilla extract. Gradually blend in the dry ingredients.

4 Spread the mixture evenly into the prepared baking pan. Sprinkle the walnuts over the top.

5 Bake for 20 to 25 minutes, until a toothpick inserted in the center comes out clean. Cool in the pan on a wire rack before cutting into large or small bars.

Cocoa Indians

Bar Cookies
YIELD: *1 to 2 dozen*
TOTAL TIME: *35 minutes*

1 cup all-purpose flour
¼ cup unsweetened cocoa powder
¼ teaspoon baking powder
¼ teaspoon salt
½ cup vegetable shortening
1 cup granulated sugar
2 large eggs
¼ cup milk
1 teaspoon vanilla extract
⅔ cup raisins

1 Preheat the oven to 400 degrees. Lightly grease a 13 by 9 inch baking pan.

2 Combine the flour, cocoa, baking powder, and salt.

3 In a large bowl, cream the vegetable shortening and sugar. Beat in the eggs. Beat in the milk and vanilla extract. Gradually blend in the dry ingredients. Fold in the raisins

4 Spread the mixture evenly in the prepared baking pan.

5 Bake for 20 to 25 minutes, until a toothpick inserted inserted in the center comes out clean. Cool slightly in the pan before cutting into large or small bars.

Cocoa Molasses Bars

Bar Cookies

YIELD: *1 to 4 dozen*
TOTAL TIME: *35–40 minutes*

2 cups all-purpose flour
¼ cup unsweetened cocoa powder
1 teaspoon baking powder
1 teaspoon ground cinnamon
1 teaspoon ground allspice
½ teaspoon ground nutmeg
½ teaspoon salt
3 large eggs
2 cups packed dark brown sugar
¼ cup molasses
2 tablespoons rum
1 teaspoon vanilla extract
1½ cups pecans, chopped

1 Preheat the oven to 325 degrees. Lightly grease a 13 by 9-inch baking pan.

2 Combine the flour, cocoa, baking powder, spices, and salt.

3 In a large bowl, beat the eggs until thick and light-colored. Beat in the brown sugar. Beat in the molasses, rum, and vanilla extract. Gradually blend in the dry ingredients. Fold in the pecans. Spread the batter evenly in the prepared baking pan.

4 Bake for 25 to 30 minutes, until the top looks dry and a toothpick inserted into the center comes out clean. Cool in the pan on a wire rack before cutting into large or small bars.

Coconut Bars

Bar Cookies

YIELD: *1 to 2 dozen*
TOTAL TIME: *30 minutes*

2 cups all-purpose flour
1½ teaspoons baking soda
¾ cup vegetable shortening
½ cup packed light brown sugar
1 cup unsweetened applesauce
½ teaspoon vanilla extract
2 cups flaked coconut
½ cup shredded coconut

1 Preheat the oven to 350 degrees. Lightly grease a 13 by 9-inch baking pan.

2 Combine the flour and baking soda.

3 In a large bowl, cream the vegetable shortening and brown sugar. Beat in the applesauce and vanilla extract. Fold in the flaked coconut.

4 Spread the dough evenly in the prepared baking pan. Sprinkle the shredded coconut on top.

5 Bake for 18 to 20 minutes, until the top is lightly colored. Cool in the pan on a wire rack before cutting into large or small bars.

Baking notes: For an added touch, drizzle White Sugar Icing over the top before cutting into bars (see Pantry).

Coconut Brownies

Bar Cookies

YIELD: *1 to 2 dozen*
TOTAL TIME: *45 minutes*

¾ cup all-purpose flour
½ teaspoon baking powder
¼ teaspoon salt
½ cup vegetable shortening
1 cup granulated sugar
2 large eggs
1½ tablespoons chocolate syrup
1 teaspoon vanilla extract
1 cup grated fresh (or packaged) coconut

1 Preheat the oven to 400 degrees. Lightly grease a 9-inch square baking pan.

2 Combine the flour, baking powder, and salt.

3 In a large bowl, cream the vegetable shortening and sugar. Beat in the eggs. Beat in the chocolate syrup and vanilla extract. Gradually blend in the dry ingredients. Fold in the coconut. Spread the mixture evenly in the prepared baking pan.

4 Bake for 30 to 35 minutes, until a toothpick inserted in the center comes out clean. Cool in the pan on a wire rack before cutting into large or small bars.

Coconut-Caramel Bars

Bar Cookies

YIELD: *1 to 2 dozen*
TOTAL TIME: *55 minutes*

CRUST
½ cup vegetable shortening
½ cup powdered sugar
1 cup all-purpose flour

TOPPING
One 14-ounce can sweetened condensed milk
1 cup (6 ounces) butterscotch chips
1 cup flaked coconut
1 teaspoon vanilla extract

1 Preheat the oven to 350 degrees. Lightly grease a 9-inch square baking pan.

2 To make the crust, cream the vegetable shortening and powdered sugar in a medium bowl. Gradually work in the flour. Press the mixture evenly into the prepared baking pan.

3 Bake for 14 minutes.

4 Meanwhile, make the topping: In a large bowl, combine the condensed milk, butterscotch chips, coconut, and vanilla extract and stir until well blended.

5 Pour the topping mixture over the hot crust. Bake for 25 to 30 minutes longer, until a toothpick inserted in the center comes out clean. Cool in the pan on a wire rack before cutting into large or small bars.

Coconut Chewies

Bar Cookies

YIELD: *1 to 2 dozen*
TOTAL TIME: *35 minutes*

2 cups all-purpose flour
1 teaspoon baking powder
½ teaspoon salt
⅔ cup vegetable shortening
2 cups packed light brown sugar
3 large eggs
1 teaspoon vanilla extract
1½ cups (9 ounces) semisweet
    chocolate chips
¾ cup walnuts, chopped
½ cup shredded coconut

1 Preheat the oven to 350 degrees. Lightly grease a 9-inch square baking pan.

2 Combine the flour, baking powder, and salt.

3 In a large bowl, cream the vegetable shortening and brown sugar. Beat in the eggs. Beat in the vanilla extract. Gradually blend in the dry ingredients. Fold in the chocolate chips, walnuts, and coconut. Spread the mixture evenly in the prepared baking pan.

4 Bake for 20 to 25 minutes, until firm to the touch. Cool in the pan on a wire rack before cutting into large or small bars.

Coconut Chews

Bar Cookies

YIELD: *2 to 3 dozen*
TOTAL TIME: *45 minutes*

CRUST
¾ teaspoon vegetable shortening
3 tablespoons granulated sugar
1½ cups whole wheat flour

TOPPING
2 large eggs
1 cup almonds, chopped
1 cup flaked coconut

1 Preheat the oven to 375 degrees. Lightly grease a 13 by 9-inch baking pan.

2 To make the crust, cream the vegetable shortening and sugar in a medium bowl. Gradually blend in the flour. Press the mixture evenly into the bottom of the prepared baking pan.

3 Bake for 15 minutes.

4 Meanwhile, prepare the topping: In a large bowl, beat the eggs with the almonds and coconut.

5 Spread the topping over the hot crust and bake for 20 minutes longer, until set. Cool in the pan on a wire rack before cutting into large or small bars.

Coconut-Pineapple Squares

Bar Cookies

Yield: *1 to 3 dozen*
Total time: *30 minutes*

2½ cups all-purpose flour
2 teaspoons baking powder
1 teaspoon baking soda
1 teaspoon ground cinnamon
½ cup vegetable shortening
3 large eggs
1 cup pineapple juice
2 cups flaked coconut
One 20-ounce can crushed pine-
    apple, drained
½ cup shredded coconut

1 Preheat the oven to 350
degrees. Lightly grease a 13 by 9-
inch baking pan.

2 Combine the flour, baking
powder, baking soda, and
cinnamon.

3 In a large bowl, beat the vegetable shortening, eggs, and
pineapple juice. Gradually blend
in the dry ingredients. Fold in the
flaked coconut and pineapple.

4 Spread the mixture evenly in
the prepared baking pan.

5 Bake for 15 minutes. Sprinkle
the shredded coconut over the
top and bake for 10 to 15 minutes
longer, until coconut is lightly
colored. Cool in the pan on a
wire rack before cutting into
large or small bars.

Coffee-Flavored Brownies

Bar Cookies

Yield: *1 to 2 dozen*
Total time: *35 minutes*

¾ cup all-purpose flour
½ teaspoon baking powder
2 tablespoons instant coffee
    crystals
¼ teaspoon salt
2 ounces unsweetened chocolate,
    chopped
⅓ cup vegetable shortening
2 large eggs
1 teaspoon vanilla extract
1 cup granulated sugar
½ cup walnuts, chopped

1 Preheat the oven to 375
degrees. Lightly grease an 8-inch
square baking pan.

2 Combine the flour, baking
powder, coffee crystals, and salt.

3 In the top of a double boiler,
melt the chocolate and shortening over low heat, stirring until
smooth. Remove from the heat.

4 In a large bowl, beat the eggs
until thick and light-colored.
Gradually beat in the chocolate
mixture and vanilla extract. Beat
in the sugar. Gradually blend in
the dry ingredients. Stir in the
walnuts.

5 Spread the batter evenly in the
prepared baking pans.

6 Bake for 20 to 25 minutes, until
a toothpick inserted in the center
comes out clean. Cool in the pan
on a wire rack before cutting into
large or small bars.

COFFEE SQUARES

Bar Cookies

YIELD: 2 to 3 dozen
TOTAL TIME: 35 minutes

1½ cups all-purpose flour
1 teaspoon baking powder
¼ teaspoon baking soda
½ teaspoon ground cardamom
¼ teaspoon salt
½ cup milk
2 teaspoons instant coffee crystals
¼ cup vegetable shortening
1 cup granulated sugar
1 cup powdered sugar
1 large egg
1 cup almonds, chopped
1 recipe for Vanilla Icing (see Pantry)

1 Preheat the oven to 350 degrees. Lightly grease a 13 by 9-inch baking pan.

2 Combine the flour, baking powder, baking soda, cardamom, and salt.

3 Combine milk and coffee crystals in a saucepan and heat, stirring, until the coffee dissolves. Remove from the heat.

4 In a large bowl, cream the vegetable shortening and both sugars. Beat in the egg. Beat in the coffee. Gradually blend in the dry ingredients. Fold in the almonds.

5 Spread the dough evenly in the prepared baking pan.

6 Bake for 18 to 20 minutes, until a toothpick inserted in the center comes out clean. Cool in the pan on a wire rack.

7 Frost the cooled cookies with the icing and cut into large or small bars.

CRACKER BROWNIES

Bar Cookies

YIELD: 1 to 2 dozen
TOTAL TIME: 45 minutes

¾ cup vegetable shortening
1 cup granulated sugar
2 large eggs
1 teaspoon vanilla extract
2½ cups crushed honey graham crackers
2 cups miniature marshmallows
¼ cup peanuts, ground fine

TOPPING
1 cup (6 ounces) semisweet chocolate chips
¼ cup peanut butter

1 Lightly grease a 9-inch square baking pan.

2 In the top of a double boiler, melt the vegetable shortening with the sugar. Stir to dissolve the sugar. Remove from the heat and beat in the eggs one at a time. Beat in the vanilla. Return to the heat and cook, stirring, until the mixture thickens. Remove from the heat and stir in the graham crackers, marshmallows, and peanuts.

3 Spread the mixture evenly in the prepared baking pan. Refrigerate until thoroughly chilled.

4 To make the topping, melt the chocolate chips with the peanut butter in a double boiler over low heat, stirring constantly. Spread this mixture evenly over the top of the graham cracker mixture. Refrigerate until the topping is set, then and cut into large or small bars.

CRACKLE BROWNIES

Bar Cookies

YIELD: *1 to 2 dozen*
TOTAL TIME: *45 minutes*

1 cup (6 ounces) semisweet choco-
    late chips
1 cup all-purpose flour
½ teaspoon baking powder
⅓ cup vegetable shortening
¾ cup granulated sugar
2 large eggs
1 teaspoon vanilla extract
¾ cup rice krispies

TOPPING
½ cup (3 ounces) semisweet choco-
    late chips
¼ cup rice krispies

1 Preheat the oven to 350
degrees. Lightly grease an 8-inch
square baking pan.

2 Melt the chocolate chips in a
double boiler over low heat, stirring until smooth. Remove from
the heat.

3 Combine the flour and baking
powder.

4 In a large bowl, cream the vegetable shortening and sugar. Beat
in the eggs and vanilla extract.
Beat in the melted chocolate.
Gradually blend in the dry ingredients. Fold in the rice krispies.
Spread the mixture evenly in the
prepared baking pan.

5 Bake for 20 to 25 minutes, until
a toothpick inserted in the center
comes out clean.

6 For the topping, sprinkle the
chocolate chips over the top of
the warm brownies. Let sit for 1
to 2 minutes, until the chocolate
melts, then spread the chocolate
evenly over the brownies. Sprinkle the rice krispies over the top.
Cool in the pan on a wire rack
before cutting into large or small
bars.

CRANBERRY BARS

Bar Cookies

YIELD: *1 to 2 dozen*
TOTAL TIME: *45 minutes*

1½ cups all-purpose flour
1 cup almonds, ground fine
1½ teaspoons baking powder
¼ teaspoon salt
2 large eggs
1 cup granulated sugar
2 teaspoons fresh lemon juice
1 cup jellied cranberry sauce,
    chopped fine

1 Preheat the oven to 350
degrees. Lightly grease a 13 by 9-
inch baking pan.

2 Combine the flour, almonds,
baking powder, and salt.

3 In a large bowl, beat the eggs,
sugar, and lemon juice. Beat in
the cranberry sauce. Gradually
blend in the dry ingredients.
Spread the dough evenly in the
prepared baking pan.

4 Bake for 25 to 30 minutes, until
the top is lightly colored and firm
to the touch. Cut into large or
small bars and cool in the pan on
a wire rack.

CRANBERRY ORANGE BARS

Bar Cookies

YIELD: *1 to 2 dozen*
TOTAL TIME: *45 minutes*

1½ cups all-purpose flour
1 teaspoon baking powder
½ teaspoon salt
6 tablespoons vegetable shortening
¾ cup granulated sugar
2 large eggs
1 cup cranberries, chopped fine
¾ cup orange marmalade

TOPPING
2 tablespoons butter, at room temperature
1 cup powdered sugar
¼ cup pecans, ground fine
1 tablespoon milk
2 tablespoons diced cranberries

1 Preheat the oven to 350 degrees. Lightly grease a 13 by 9-inch baking pan.

2 Combine the flour, baking powder, and salt.

3 In a large bowl, cream the vegetable shortening and sugar. Beat in the eggs. Beat in the cranberries and marmalade. Gradually blend in the dry ingredients. Spread the dough evenly into the prepared baking pan.

4 Bake for 25 to 30 minutes, until firm to the touch.

5 Meanwhile, make the topping: In a medium bowl, cream the butter and powdered sugar. Beat in the pecans. Beat in the milk.

6 Spread the topping evenly over the hot cookies. Sprinkle the diced cranberries on top. Cool in the pan on a wire rack before cutting into large or small bars.

Baking notes: Refrigerate these bars once they have cooled. Serve them with whipped cream.

CREAM CHEESE BROWNIES

Bar Cookies

YIELD: *2 to 3 dozen*
TOTAL TIME: *50 minutes*

½ cup all-purpose flour
½ teaspoon baking powder
¼ teaspoon salt
⅓ cup semisweet chocolate chips
5 tablespoons vegetable shortening
1 cup granulated sugar
3 ounces cream cheese, at room temperature
3 large eggs
2 teaspoons vanilla extract
½ teaspoon almond extract
½ cup almonds, chopped

1 Preheat the oven to 350 degrees. Lightly grease a 9-inch square baking pan.

2 Combine the flour, baking powder, and salt.

3 In the top of a double boiler, melt the chocolate chips and vegetable shortening, stirring until smooth. Transfer to a large bowl.

4 Add the sugar to the chocolate mixture and beat until smooth. Beat in the cream cheese. Beat in the eggs, beating well after each addition. Beat in the vanilla and in the dry ingredients. Fold in the almonds. Scrape the batter into the prepared baking pan.

5 Bake for 35 to 40 minutes, until a toothpick inserted in the center comes out clean. Cool in the pan on a wire rack before cutting into large or small bars.

Crème de Menthe Brownies

Bar Cookies

YIELD: *1 to 2 dozen*
TOTAL TIME: *40 minutes*

½ cup plus 2 tablespoons vegetable shortening
¼ cup unsweetened cocoa powder
1 cup granulated sugar
2 large eggs
½ teaspoon crème de menthe
⅔ cup all-purpose flour
Green crème de menthe icing (see Pantry)
Walnut halves

1 Preheat the oven to 350 degrees. Lightly grease a 9-inch square baking pan.

2 Melt the vegetable shortening in a large saucepan. Beat in the cocoa powder. Remove from the heat and beat in the sugar. Beat in the eggs and crème de menthe. Gradually blend in the flour. Spread the batter evenly in the prepared baking pan.

3 Bake for 18 to 20 minutes, until a toothpick inserted into the center comes out clean. Cool in the pan on a wire rack.

4 Spread the icing over the top of the brownies and cut into large or small bars. Place a walnut half in the center of each brownie. Chill for about at least 1 hour before removing from the pan.

Crunchy Chocolate Bars

Bar Cookies

YIELD: *1 to 2 dozen*
TOTAL TIME: *30 minutes*

2 cups (12 ounces) semisweet chocolate chips
¾ cup chunky peanut butter
3 cups Cheerios

1 Grease an 8-inch square baking pan.

2 In the top of a double boiler, melt the chocolate chips with the peanut butter, stirring until smooth. Remove from the heat and gradually blend in the cereal.

3 Spread the dough evenly in the prepared baking pan. Refrigerate until thoroughly chilled, then cut into large or small bars.

CURRANT BARS

Bar Cookies

YIELD: *2 to 4 dozen*
TOTAL TIME: *35 minutes*

3 cups all-purpose flour
½ teaspoon baking soda
½ teaspoon ground cinnamon
¼ teaspoon ground cloves
½ teaspoon salt
1 cup vegetable shortening
¾ cup granulated sugar
¾ cup packed light brown sugar
2 large eggs, slightly beaten
⅓ cup orange juice
1 cup currants
1 cup flaked coconut

TOPPING
¾ cup powdered sugar
1 tablespoon plus 1 teaspoon fresh orange juice
1 teaspoon finely shredded orange zest

1 Preheat the oven to 350 degrees. Lightly grease 2 baking sheets.

2 Combine the flour, baking soda, spices, and salt.

3 Melt the vegetable shortening in a large saucepan. Remove from the heat and beat in the two sugars. Beat in the eggs one at a time. Beat in the orange juice. Gradually blend in the dry ingredients. Fold in the currants and coconut. Spread the mixture evenly in the prepared baking pan.

4 Bake for 20 to 25 minutes, until light colored on top.

5 Meanwhile, in a small bowl combine all of the ingredients for the topping and stir until smooth.

6 Spread the topping over the warm cookies. Cool in the pan on a wire rack before cutting into large or small bars.

CURRANT-RAISIN BARS

Bar Cookies

YIELD: *1 to 2 dozen*
TOTAL TIME: *35 minutes*

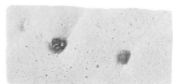

1 cup all-purpose flour
1 teaspoon baking powder
¼ teaspoon salt
2 large eggs
1 cup granulated sugar
1 teaspoon fresh lemon juice
¾ cup golden raisins
¾ cup currants

1 Preheat the oven to 350 degrees. Lightly grease a 13 by 9-inch square baking pan.

2 Combine the flour, baking powder, and salt.

3 In a large bowl, beat the eggs and sugar until thick and light-colored. Beat in the lemon juice. Gradually blend in the dry ingredients. Fold in the raisins and currants. Spread the batter evenly in the prepared baking pan.

4 Bake for 20 to 25 minutes, until a toothpick inserted in the center come out clean. Cool in the pan on a wire rack before cutting into large or small bars.

DANISH APPLE BARS

Bar Cookies

YIELD: *3 to 4 dozen*
TOTAL TIME: *60 minutes*

CRUST
2½ cups all-purpose flour
1 teaspoon salt
1 large egg yolk
⅓ cup plus 2 teaspoons milk
1 cup vegetable shortening
¾ cup granulated sugar
1 cup cornflakes
8 cups peeled, sliced apples

FILLING
1 cup powdered sugar
1 teaspoon ground cinnamon
1 large egg white, beaten
Powdered sugar for sprinkling

1 Preheat the oven to 375 degrees. Lightly grease a 15 by 10-inch baking pan.

2 To make the crust, combine the flour and salt.

3 Place the egg yolk in a measuring cup, and add enough milk to measure a ⅔ cup.

4 In a large bowl, cream the vegetable shortening and sugar. Beat in the egg yolk and milk. Gradually blend in the dry ingredients.

5 Divide the dough in half. On a floured surface, roll out half of the dough to a 16 by 11-inch rec-

tangle and fit it into the prepared baking pan.

6 Spread the cornflakes on top of the dough and arrange the apple on top of the cornflakes. Combine the powdered sugar and cinnamon and sprinkle over the apples.

7 Roll out the remaining dough to a 16 by 11-inch rectangle and place it on top of the filling. Pinch the edges of the dough together to seal. Cut 2 or 3 slits in the top for steam to escape. Brush the top with the beaten egg whites.

8 Bake for 45 to 50 minutes, until the crust is golden brown. Sprinkle with powdered sugar and cool in the pan on a wire rack before cutting into large or small bars.

DANISH APRICOT BARS

Bar Cookies

YIELD: *3 to 4 dozen*
TOTAL TIME: *60 minutes*

CRUST

2½ cups all-purpose flour
1 teaspoon salt
1 cup butter, at room temperature
¾ cup packed light brown sugar
1 large egg yolk
1 tablespoon plus ½ teaspoon sour
  milk

FILLING

1 cup rolled oats
1½ tablespoons butter, at room
  temperature
8 cups thinly sliced apricots
1 cup granulated sugar
1 teaspoon ground allspice
1 large egg white, beaten
Granulated sugar for sprinkling

1 Preheat the oven to 375 degrees. Lightly grease a 15 by 10-inch baking pan.

2 To make the crust, combine the flour and salt.

3 In a large bowl, cream the butter and brown sugar. Beat in the egg yolk and sour milk. Gradually blend in the dry ingredients.

4 Divide the dough in half. On a floured surface, roll out half of the dough to a 6 by 11-inch rectangle and fit it into the prepared baking pan.

5 Spread the oats on top of the dough and dot with butter. Arrange the apricot slices on top of the oats. Combine the sugar and allspice and sprinkle over the apricots.

6 Roll out the remaining dough to a 16 by 11-inch rectangle and place it on top of the filling. Pinch the edges of the dough to seal. Cut 2 or 3 slits in the top for steam to escape. Brush the top with the beaten egg white and sprinkle with granulated sugar.

7 Bake for 45 to 50 minutes, until the crust is golden brown. Cool in the pan on a wire rack before cutting into large or small bars.

DANISH PEACH BARS

Bar Cookies

YIELD: *1 to 2 dozen*
TOTAL TIME: *60 minutes*

CRUST
2½ cups all-purpose flour
1 teaspoon salt
1 cup butter, at room temperature
¾ cup powdered sugar
1 large egg yolk
2 ounces cream cheese, at room temperature

FILLING
1 cup wheat flake cereal, crushed
8 cups dices dried peaches
1 cup loosely packed light brown sugar
1 teaspoon ground allspice
1 large egg white, beaten
Granulated sugar for sprinkling

1 Preheat the oven to 375 degrees. Lightly grease a 15 by 10-inch baking pan.

2 To make the crust, combine the flour and salt.

3 In a large bowl, cream the butter and powdered sugar. Beat in the egg yolk. Beat in the cream cheese. Gradually blend in the dry ingredients.

4 Divide the dough in half. On a floured surface, roll out half of the dough to a 16 by 11-inch rectangle and fit it into the prepared baking pan.

5 Spread the cereal on top of the dough and layer the peaches on top of the cereal. Combine the brown sugar and allspice and sprinkle over the peaches.

6 Roll out the remaining dough to a 16 by 11-inch rectangle and place it on top of the filling. Pinch the edges of the dough to seal. Cut 2 or 3 slits in the top for steam to escape. Brush the top with the beaten egg white and sprinkle with granulated sugar.

7 Bake for 45 to 50 minutes, until the crust is golden brown. Cool in the pan on a wire rack before cutting into large or small bars.

DARK SECRETS

Bar Cookies

YIELD: *6 to 7 dozen*
TOTAL TIME: *35 minutes*

5 cups all-purpose flour
1 teaspoon baking powder
¼ teaspoon salt
2 tablespoons vegetable shortening
¾ cup granulated sugar
¼ cup packed light brown sugar
3 large eggs
1 teaspoon rum
1 cup dates, pitted and chopped
1 cup pecans, chopped
Powdered sugar for rolling

1 Preheat the oven to 350 degrees. Lightly grease a 15 by 10-inch baking pan.

2 Combine the flour, baking powder, and salt.

3 In a large bowl, cream the vegetable shortening and two sugars. Beat in the eggs one at a time. Beat in the rum. Gradually blend in the dry ingredients. Fold in the dates and pecans. Spread the dough evenly in the prepared baking pan.

4 Bake for 15 to 20 minutes, until just lightly colored; do not overbake. Cool slightly in the pan on a wire rack.

5 Cut the warm cookies into 2 by 1-inch strips and roll them in powdered sugar.

DATE BARS

Bar Cookies

YIELD: *1 to 2 dozen*
TOTAL TIME: *35 minutes*

½ cup all-purpose flour
½ teaspoon baking powder
Pinch of salt
⅔ cup sweetened condensed milk
½ teaspoon vanilla extract
½ cup dates, pitted and chopped
¼ cup walnuts, chopped

1 Preheat the oven to 375 degrees. Lightly grease a 9-inch square baking pan.

2 Combine the flour, baking powder, and salt.

3 In a medium bowl, beat the condensed milk and vanilla extract together. Gradually blend in the dry ingredients. Stir in the dates and walnuts. Spread the mixture evenly in the prepared baking pan.

4 Bake for 18 to 20 minutes, until lightly colored on top. Cool in the pan on a wire rack before cutting into large or small bars.

DATE BROWNIES

Bar Cookies

YIELD: *1 to 3 dozen*
TOTAL TIME: *35 minutes*

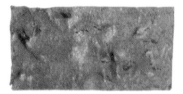

½ cup all-purpose flour
¼ teaspoon baking powder
¼ teaspoon salt
2 ounces bittersweet chocolate, chopped
½ cup vegetable shortening
1 cup granulated sugar
2 large eggs
1 teaspoon vanilla extract
1 cup walnuts, chopped
⅔ cup dates, pitted and chopped

1 Preheat the oven to 325 degrees. Lightly grease a 9-inch square baking pan.

2 Combine the flour, baking powder, and salt.

3 In the top of a double boiler, melt the chocolate and vegetable shortening, stirring until smooth. Remove from the heat and beat in the sugar. Beat in the eggs one at a time. Beat in the vanilla extract. Gradually blend in the dry ingredients. Stir in the walnuts and dates. Spread the mixture evenly in the prepared baking pan.

4 Bake for 20 to 25 minutes, or until a toothpick inserted in the center comes out clean. Cool in the pan on a wire rack before cutting into large or small bars.

DATE-GRANOLA SQUARES

Bar Cookies

YIELD: *1 to 3 dozen*

2½ cups all purpose flour
2 teaspoons baking powder
½ teaspoon baking soda
1 teaspoon ground cinnamon
½ teaspoon ground nutmeg
¼ teaspoon ground ginger
¼ teaspoon salt
½ cup canola oil
2 large eggs
1½ cup pear juice
1 cup unsweetened granola (see Baking notes)
1 cup dates, pitted and chopped

TOPPING
½ cup dates, pitted and chopped very fine
½ cup unsweetened granola

1 Preheat the oven to 350 degrees. Lightly grease a 13 by 9-inch baking pan.

2 Combine the flour, baking powder, baking soda, spices, and salt.

3 In a large bowl, beat the canola oil and eggs together. Beat in the pear juice. Gradually blend in the dry ingredients. Stir in the granola and dates. Spread the mixture evenly in the prepared baking pan.

4 To make the topping, combine the dates and granola in a small bowl and toss to mix. Sprinkle evenly over the top of the granola mixture.

5 Bake for 25 to 30 minutes, until firm to the touch. Cool in the pan on a wire rack before cutting into large or small bars.

Baking notes: If you wish to make your own granola, combine equal amounts of rolled oats, chopped nuts, flaked coconut, sesame seeds, chopped sunflower seeds, and chopped dried fruit, such as banana chips and/or raisins.

Date-Honey Fingers

Bar Cookies

YIELD: *4 to 5 dozen*
TOTAL TIME: *40 minutes*

¾ cup all purpose flour
½ teaspoon baking powder
Pinch of salt
¼ cup butter, at room temperature
5 tablespoons honey
2 large eggs
⅔ cup dates, pitted and chopped
½ cup walnuts, chopped fine
Powdered sugar for sprinkling

1 Preheat the oven to 375 degrees. Lightly grease an 8-inch square baking pan.

2 Combine the flour, baking powder, and salt.

3 In a large bowl, beat the butter and honey until smooth. Beat in the eggs. Gradually blend in the dry ingredients. Fold in the dates and walnuts. Spread the dough evenly in the prepared baking pan.

4 Bake for 25 to 30 minutes, until firm to the touch. Cool in the pan on a wire rack.

5 Sprinkle the cookies with powdered sugar and cut into finger-sized bars.

Date-Nut Fingers

Formed Cookies

YIELD: *4 to 5 dozen*
TOTAL TIME: *50 minutes*

1¼ cups toasted rice cereal
1 cup dates, pitted and chopped fine
1 cup pecans, chopped
½ cup butter
¼ cup granulated sugar
¼ cup packed light brown sugar
1 large egg
1 cup shredded coconut

1 Combine the cereal, dates, and pecans in a large bowl.

2 Combine the butter and two sugars in the top of a double boiler and cook over low heat, stirring, until the butter melts and the sugar dissolves. Beat in the egg and cook for 20 minutes, stirring occasionally, until very thick. Do not allow the mixture to boil.

3 Pour the hot sugar mixture over the date mixture and stir to coat well. Let cool slightly.

4 Pinch off pieces of dough and form into 2 by 1-inch strips. Roll the strips in the shredded coconut and let cool.

DELICIOUS FUDGE BROWNIES

Bar Cookies

YIELD: *1 to 2 dozen*
TOTAL TIME: *45 minutes*

1⅓ cups all-purpose flour
¾ cup unsweetened cocoa powder
¼ teaspoon salt
⅔ cup vegetable oil
2 cups granulated sugar
2 large eggs
1 teaspoon vanilla extract
½ cup walnuts, chopped

1 Preheat the oven to 350 degrees. Lightly grease a 13 by 9-inch baking pan.

2 Combine the flour, cocoa powder, and salt.

3 In a large bowl, beat the vegetable oil and sugar. Beat in the eggs one at a time. Beat in the vanilla extract. Gradually blend in the dry ingredients. Fold in the walnuts. Spread the mixture evenly in the prepared baking pan.

4 Bake for 25 to 30 minutes, or until a toothpick inserted in the center comes out clean. Cool in the pan on a wire rack before cutting into large or small bars.

Baking notes: For a more decorative appearance, sprinkle the walnuts on top of the batter before baking.

DUTCH-CRUNCH APPLESAUCE BARS

Bar Cookies

YIELD: *1 to 2 dozen*
TOTAL TIME: *40 minutes*

2 cups all-purpose flour
1 teaspoon baking soda
1 teaspoon ground cinnamon
½ teaspoon ground nutmeg
¼ teaspoon salt
1 cup granulated sugar
1 cup unsweetened applesauce
1 teaspoon vanilla extract
½ cup walnuts, chopped

TOPPING
2 tablespoons butter, at room temperature
¼ cup granulated sugar
⅔ cup crushed breakfast cereal (such as cornflakes)

1 Preheat the oven to 350 degrees. Lightly grease a 13 by 9-inch baking pan.

2 Combine the flour, baking soda, spices, and salt.

3 In a large bowl, beat the sugar, applesauce, and vanilla extract. Gradually blend in the dry ingredients. Stir in the walnuts. Spread the mixture evenly in the prepared baking pan.

4 To make the topping cream the butter and sugar in a small bowl. Gradually blend in the cereal. Spread this over the dough.

5 Bake for 20 to 30 minutes, until lightly browned on top. Cool in the pan on a wire rack before cutting into large or small bars.

Dutch Tea Cakes

Bar Cookies

Yield: *3 to 4 dozen*
Total time: *2 hours*

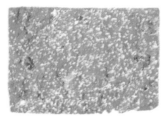

4 cups all-purpose flour
1 cup packed light brown sugar
1 teaspoon baking powder
1 teaspoon ground cinnamon
½ teaspoon ground cloves
1 cup candied citrus peel, chopped
 fine
1 cup milk
1 cup molasses
Powdered sugar for sprinkling

1 Preheat the oven to 300
degrees. Lightly grease a 9-inch
square baking pan.

2 In a large bowl, combine the
flour, brown sugar, baking powder, spices, and candied peel.
Gradually stir in the milk and
molasses. Spread the dough
evenly in the prepared baking
pan.

3 Bake for 1½ to 2 hours, or until
firm and the top looks dry. Place
a paper doily on top of the hot
cookies and sprinkle with sugar.
Let cool on a rack before cutting
into large or small bars.

English Toffee Bars

Bar Cookies

Yield: *1 to 2 dozen*
Total time: *75 minutes*

2 cups all-purpose flour
1 teaspoon ground cinnamon
1 cup vegetable shortening
1 cup packed light brown sugar
1 large egg yolk
1 cup black or regular walnuts,
 chopped

1 Preheat the oven to 275
degrees. Lightly grease a 9-inch
square baking pan.

2 Combine the flour and
cinnamon.

3 In a large bowl, cream the vegetable shortening and brown
sugar. Beat in the egg yolk. Gradually blend in the dry ingredients. Fold in the walnuts. Spread
the mixture evenly in the prepared baking pan.

4 Bake for 55 to 60 minutes, until
firm to the touch. Cool in the pan
on a wire rack before cutting into
large or small bars.

FRESH PLUM BARS

Bar Cookies

YIELD: *1 to 3 dozen*
TOTAL TIME: *55 minutes*

CRUST
1½ cups all-purpose flour
¼ teaspoon salt
½ cup vegetable shortening
¼ cup granulated sugar
1 large egg yolk
4 cups pitted plums, sliced
½ cup powdered sugar

FILLING
8 ounces cream cheese, at room temperature
¾ cup sour cream
3 large eggs
¾ cup powdered sugar
½ teaspoon grated lemon zest
1 teaspoon almond extract
1 teaspoon ground cinnamon
¼ teaspoon ground cloves

1 Preheat the oven to 350 degrees. Lightly grease a 9-inch square baking pan.

2 To make the crust, combine the flour and salt.

3 In a large bowl, cream the vegetable shortening and sugar. Beat in the egg yolk. Gradually blend in the dry ingredients. Spread the dough evenly in the prepared baking pan.

4 Arrange the sliced plums on top of the dough. Sprinkle the powdered sugar over the plums. Bake for 15 minutes.

5 Meanwhile, make the filling: In a large bowl, combine the cream cheese, sour cream, eggs, powdered sugar, lemon zest, almond extract, and spices and beat until smooth.

6 Spread the topping evenly over the hot crust. Bake for 30 to 35 minutes longer, or until firm to the touch. Cool in the pan on a wire rack before cutting into large or small bars, then refrigerate until ready to serve.

Baking notes: These bars should be served well chilled, with a dab of whipped cream on top.

Fruit Bars

Bar Cookies

YIELD: *1 to 4 dozen*
TOTAL TIME: *45 minutes*
CHILLING TIME: *8 hours*

---

3 cups all-purpose flour
1 teaspoon baking soda
½ teaspoon ground cinnamon
¼ teaspoon ground nutmeg
¼ teaspoon ground cloves
¼ teaspoon ground ginger
½ teaspoon salt
¾ cup vegetable shortening
1 cup granulated sugar
¼ cup white port
1 cup evaporated milk
½ cup finely chopped candied citron
¼ cup finely chopped candied
    pineapple
¼ cup finely chopped candied
    cherries
¼ cup finely chopped candied
    orange peel
1 tablespoon grated lemon zest
½ cup walnuts, chopped

1 Combine the flour, baking soda, spices, and salt.

2 In a large bowl, cream the vegetable shortening and sugar. Beat in the port. Beat in the milk. Gradually blend in the dry ingredients. Fold in the candied fruit and lemon zest. Stir in the walnuts. Cover and chill for 8 hours or overnight.

3 Preheat the oven to 350 degrees.

4 Spread the dough evenly in an ungreased 13 by 9-inch baking pan. Bake for 25 to 30 minutes, until golden on top.

5 Cool in the pan on a wire rack before cutting into large or small bars.

Baking notes: These are good frosted with Rum Buttercream (see Pantry). Store these bars tightly covered.

Fruit-Filled Oatcakes

Bar Cookies

YIELD: *1 to 3 dozen*
TOTAL TIME: *45 minutes*

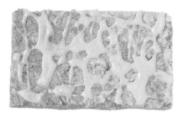

1½ cups all-purpose flour
1½ cups rolled oats
½ teaspoon baking soda
½ teaspoon salt
½ cup vegetable shortening
1 cup packed light brown sugar
Fruit filling (your choice of jam or
    preserves)

1 Preheat the oven to 350 degrees. Lightly grease a 13 by 9-inch baking pan.

2 Cream the flour, rolled oats, baking soda, and salt.

3 In a large bowl, cream the vegetable shortening and brown sugar. Gradually blend in the dry ingredients.

4 Spread half of the dough evenly into the prepared pan. Spread the fruit filling over the dough and press the remaining dough over the top of the fruit.

5 Bake for 20 to 25 minutes, until lightly colored on top. Cool in the pan on a wire rack before cutting into large or small bars.

Baking notes: You can dress up these bars with a drizzle of white or lemon frosting (see Pantry).

FRUIT MERINGUE BARS

Bar Cookies

YIELD: *1 to 4 dozen*
TOTAL TIME: *45 minutes*

CRUST
¾ cup vegetable shortening
¼ cup granulated sugar
2 large egg yolks
1½ cups all-purpose flour

TOPPING
2 large egg whites, beaten
½ cup granulated sugar
1 cup almonds, chopped

FILLING
1 cup raspberry puree (see Baking notes)
1 cup flaked coconut

1 Preheat the oven to 350 degrees. Lightly grease a 13 by 9-inch baking pan.

2 To make the crust, cream the vegetable shortening and sugar in a medium bowl. Beat in the egg yolks. Gradually blend in the flour. Press the dough evenly into the prepared baking pan.

3 Bake for 15 minutes.

4 Meanwhile, make the topping: In a medium bowl, beat the egg whites until foamy. Fold in the sugar and almonds.

5 Spread the raspberry puree over the hot crust. Sprinkle the coconut over the puree. Spread the topping over the coconut.

6 Bake for 20 to 25 minutes longer until the topping is set and lightly colored. Cool in a pan on a wire rack before cutting into large or small bars.

Baking notes: To make raspberry puree, place drained, frozen raspberries in a blender and puree.

FUDGE BROWNIES I

Bar Cookies

YIELD: *1 to 2 dozen*
TOTAL TIME: *45 minutes*

½ cup vegetable shortening
2 ounces semisweet chocolate, chopped
2 cups granulated sugar
4 large egg yolks
1¼ teaspoons vanilla extract
1 cup all-purpose flour
1 cup walnuts, chopped

1 Preheat the oven to 325 degrees. Lightly grease a 9-inch square baking pan.

2 In the top of a double boiler, melt the vegetable shortening and chocolate, stirring until smooth. Remove from the heat and beat in the sugar. Beat in the egg yolks one at a time. Beat in the vanilla extract. Gradually blend in the flour. Fold in the nuts. Spread the batter evenly in the prepared baking pan.

3 Bake for 25 to 30 minutes, until a toothpick inserted in the center comes out clean. Cool in the pan on a wire rack before cutting into large or small bars.

Baking notes: Frost before cutting into bars if you wish (see Pantry).

Fudge Brownies II

Bar Cookies

YIELD: *1 to 2 dozen*
TOTAL TIME: *45 minutes*

1⅓ cups all-purpose flour
¾ cup unsweetened, cocoa powder
¼ teaspoon salt
⅔ cup vegetable oil
2 cups granulated sugar
2 large eggs
1 teaspoon almond extract
½ cup almonds, chopped

1 Preheat the oven to 350 degrees. Lightly grease a 13 by 9-inch square baking pan.

2 Combine the flour, cocoa powder, and salt.

3 In a large bowl, beat the vegetable oil and sugar together. Beat in the eggs one at a time. Beat in the almond extract. Gradually blend in the dry ingredients. Stir in the almonds. Spread the mixture evenly into the prepared baking pan.

4 Bake for 25 to 30 minutes, until a toothpick inserted into the center comes out clean. Cool in the pan on a wire rack before cutting into large or small bars.

Baking notes: Frost before cutting if you wish (see Pantry).

Fudge Brownies III

Bar Cookies

YIELD: *1 to 2 dozen*
TOTAL TIME: *45 minutes*

¾ cup all-purpose flour
½ teaspoon baking powder
½ teaspoon salt
6 ounces bittersweet chocolate, chopped
⅓ cup vegetable shortening
1 cup granulated sugar
2 large eggs
½ cup walnuts, chopped

1 Preheat the oven to 350 degrees. Lightly grease a 9-inch square baking pan.

2 Combine the flour, baking powder, and salt.

3 In the top of a double boiler, melt the chocolate and vegetable shortening, stirring until smooth. Remove from the heat and beat in the sugar. Beat in the eggs one at a time. Gradually blend in the dry ingredients. Fold in the walnuts.

4 Spread the batter evenly in the prepared pan.

5 Bake for 30 to 35 minutes, until a toothpick inserted in the center comes out clean. Cool in the pan on a wire rack before cutting into large or small bars.

Baking notes: Frost before cutting into bars if you like (see Pantry).

FUDGIES

Drop Cookies
YIELD: *4 to 6 dozen*
TOTAL TIME: *30 minutes*

2 cups all-purpose flour
½ cup unsweetened cocoa powder
½ teaspoon baking soda
¼ teaspoon salt
¼ cup vegetable shortening
½ cup granulated sugar
1 large egg
½ cup buttermilk
½ cup molasses
1 teaspoon vanilla extract
¾ cup walnuts, chopped

1 Preheat the oven to 350 degrees. Lightly grease 2 baking sheets.

2 Combine the flour, cocoa powder, baking soda, and salt.

3 In a large bowl, cream the vegetable shortening and sugar. Beat in the egg. Beat in the buttermilk and molasses. Beat in the vanilla extract. Gradually blend in the dry ingredients. Fold in the walnuts.

4 Drop the dough by spoonfuls 1½ inches apart onto the prepared baking sheets.

5 Bake for 12 to 15 minutes, until firm to the touch. Transfer to wire racks to cool.

Baking notes: Sour milk can be used in place of the buttermilk.

GERMAN BROWNIES

Bar Cookies
YIELD: *1 to 2 dozen*
TOTAL TIME: *45 minutes*

½ cup all-purpose flour
½ cup walnuts, ground
½ teaspoon baking powder
¼ teaspoon salt
5 tablespoons vegetable shortening
4 tablespoons semisweet chocolate
3 ounces cream cheese, at room temperature
1 cup granulated sugar
3 large eggs
½ teaspoon almond extract

1 Preheat the oven to 350 degrees. Lightly grease a 9-inch square baking pan.

2 Combine the flour, walnuts, baking powder, and salt.

3 In the top of a double boiler, melt 3 tablespoons of the vegetable shortening and the chocolate, stirring until smooth. Remove from the heat and beat in the remaining 2 tablespoons shortening and the cream cheese. Beat in the sugar. Beat in the eggs and almond extract. Gradually blend in the dry ingredients. Spread the batter evenly in the prepared baking pan.

4 Bake for 12 to 15 minutes, or until a toothpick inserted in the center comes out clean. Cool in the pan on a wire rack before cutting into large or small bars.

Baking notes: Frost these with chocolate icing to make them even more indulgent.

GERMAN HONEY COOKIES

Bar Cookies

YIELD: *5 to 7 dozen*
TOTAL TIME: *75 minutes*

CRUST
1¾ cups all-purpose flour
¼ cup granulated sugar
1 cup almonds, ground fine
2 teaspoons baking powder
¼ teaspoon salt
½ cup vegetable shortening

TOPPING
½ cup vegetable shortening
½ cup granulated sugar
1 large egg
2 tablespoons honey
2 tablespoons milk
1 teaspoon vanilla extract
2 tablespoons almond extract

1 Preheat the oven to 350 degrees.

2 To make the crust, combine the flour, sugar, almonds, baking powder, and salt in a large bowl. Cut inthe vegetable shortening until the mixture resembles coarse crumbs. Press the mixture evenly into an ungreased 9-inch square baking pan.

3 To make the topping, combine the vegetable shortening, sugar, egg, honey, and milk in a saucepan and bring to a boil. Remove from the heat and stir in the almond and vanilla extracts. Let cool slightly.

4 Pour the topping over the crust. Bake for 55 to 60 minutes, until lightly colored on top and firm to the touch. Cool in the pan on a wire rack before cutting into large or small bars.

Baking notes: Older versions of this recipe call for buttermilk or sour milk in place of the whole milk. Others use hazelnuts instead of almonds and schnapps instead of the almond extract. These are traditionally cut into squares or triangles.

Ginger Bars

Bar Cookies

YIELD: *1 to 4 dozen*
TOTAL TIME: *35 minutes*

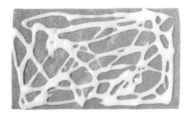

1½ cups all-purpose flour
½ teaspoon ground cinnamon
½ teaspoon ground ginger
½ teaspoon ground nutmeg
½ teaspoon salt
½ teaspoon baking soda
½ cup hot water
½ cup butter, at room temperature
½ cup packed light brown sugar
2 large eggs
½ cup molasses
Vanilla Icing (see Pantry)

1 Preheat the oven to 350 degrees. Lightly grease a 13 by 9-inch baking pan.

2 Combine the flour, spices, and salt.

3 In a small bowl, dissolve the baking soda in the hot water. Stir in the molasses.

4 In a large bowl, cream the butter and brown sugar. Beat in the eggs. Beat in the molasses mixture. Gradually blend in the dry ingredients. Spread the dough evenly in the prepared baking pan.

5 Bake for 18 to 20 minutes, or until a toothpick inserted in the center comes out clean.

6 Frost the warm cookies with icing. Let cool before cutting into large or smalls.

Ginger Creams

Bar Cookies

YIELD: *8 to 9 dozen*
TOTAL TIME: *25 minutes*

3½ cups all-purpose flour
2 teaspoons baking soda
1 teaspoon ground ginger
1 teaspoon ground cinnamon
½ teaspoon salt
1 cup vegetable shortening
1 cup molasses
½ cup granulated sugar
2 large egg yolks
½ cup milk
1 cup raisins

1 Preheat the oven to 350 degrees. Grease a 15 by 10-inch baking pan.

2 Combine the flour, baking soda, spices, and salt.

3 In a large saucepan, melt the vegetable shortening with the molasses. Remove from the heat and beat in the sugar. Beat in the egg yolks. Beat in the milk. Gradually blend in the dry ingredients. Stir in the raisins. Spread the batter evenly in the prepared baking pan.

4 Bake for 12 to 15 minutes, until lightly colored. Cool in the pan on a wire rack before cutting into large or small squares.

GRAHAM CRACKER BROWNIES I

Bar Cookies

YIELD: *1 to 2 dozen*
TOTAL TIME: *35 minutes*

1½ cups graham cracker crumbs
¾ cup semisweet chocolate chips
½ cup almonds, chopped
½ cup shredded coconut
One 14-ounce can sweetened con-
    densed milk

1 Preheat the oven to 350
degrees. Lightly grease a 9-inch
square baking pan.

2 In a large bowl, combine all of
the ingredients and blend well.
Spread the mixture evenly in the
prepared baking pan.

3 Bake for 20 to 25 minutes, until
firm to the touch. Cool in the pan
on a wire rack before cutting into
large or small bars.

GRAHAM CRACKER BROWNIES II

Bar Cookies

YIELD: *1 to 2 dozen*
TOTAL TIME: *25 minutes*
CHILLING TIME: *2 hours*

¾ cup vegetable shortening
¼ cup peanut butter
1 cup granulated sugar
2 large eggs
2½ cups graham crackers crumbs
2 cups miniature marshmallows
1 teaspoon vanilla extract

TOPPING
1 cup (6 ounces) semisweet choco-
    late chips
¼ cup peanuts, ground fine

1 Lightly grease a 9-inch square
baking pan.

2 In the top of a double boiler,
melt the vegetable shortening
with the peanut butter. Beat in
the sugar. Remove from the heat
and beat in the eggs one at a
time. Return to the heat and
cook, stirring, until the mixture
thickens. Remove from the heat
and stir in the graham crackers,
marshmallows, and vanilla
extract.

3 Spread the mixture evenly into
the prepared baking pan. Chill
for 2 hours.

4 To make the topping, melt the
chocolate chips in a double boiler
over low heat, stirring until
smooth. Remove from the heat
and stir in the ground peanuts.

5 Spread the topping evenly
over the chilled brownies. Chill
for 1 hour before cutting into
large or small bars.

Granola Bars

Bar Cookies

Yield: 3 to 4 dozen
Total time: 50 minutes

6 cups rolled oats
1 cup shredded coconut
1 cup wheat germ
1 cup golden raisins
½ cup sunflower seeds
¼ cup sesame seeds, toasted
1 teaspoon ground allspice
1 cup honey
¾ cup canola oil
⅓ cup water
1½ teaspoons vanilla extract

1 Preheat the oven to 350 degrees. Lightly grease a 13 by 9-inch baking pan.

2 Combine the oats, coconut, wheat germ, raisins, sunflower seeds, sesame seeds, and allspice in a large bowl.

3 In a saucepan, combine the honey, oil, and water and heat. Remove from the heat and stir in the vanilla extract. Add to the dry ingredients and stir to coat well. Spread the mixture evenly in the prepared baking pan.

4 Bake for 30 to 40 minutes, until firm to the touch and no longer sticky. Transfer to wire racks to cool before cutting into large or small bars.

5 To store, wrap the bars individually in waxed paper.

Grape Bars

Bar Cookies

Yield: 1 to 3 dozen
Total time: 45 minutes

Crust
1½ cups all-purpose flour
½ teaspoon baking soda
½ teaspoon salt
¾ cup vegetable shortening
1 cup granulated sugar

Topping
1½ cups dried apricots, chopped fine
½ cup dates, pitted and chopped
½ cup grape jelly
¼ cup fresh orange juice
½ cup walnuts, grounds
1½ cups rolled oats

1 Preheat the oven to 350 degrees. Lightly grease a 13 by 9-inch baking pan.

2 To make the crust, combine the flour, baking soda, and salt.

3 In a large bowl, cream the vegetable shortening and sugar. Gradually blend in the dry ingredients. Spread the mixture evenly in the prepared baking pan.

4 Bake for 20 minutes.

5 Meanwhile, make the topping: In a saucepan, combine the apricots, dates, grape jelly, orange juice, and walnuts and cook until soft. Remove from the heat.

6 Spread the topping over the hot crust. Sprinkle the oats evenly over the top and press down lightly.

7 Bake for 10 minutes longer, or until lightly colored. Transfer to wire racks to cool before cutting into large or small bars.

GRAPEFRUIT BARS

Bar Cookies

YIELD: *1 to 3 dozen*
TOTAL TIME: *35 minutes*

2 cups all-purpose flour
1 teaspoon baking soda
1 teaspoon ground cinnamon
½ teaspoon salt
¾ cup vegetable shortening
1½ cups packed light brown sugar
2 large eggs
3 tablespoons fresh grapefruit juice
3 tablespoons grated grapefruit zest

1 Preheat the oven to 350 degrees. Lightly grease a 9-inch square baking pan.

2 Combine the flour, baking soda, cinnamon, and salt.

3 In a large bowl, cream the vegetable shortening and brown sugar. Beat in the eggs. Beat in the grapefruit juice and zest. Gradually blend in the dry ingredients. Spread the batter evenly into the prepared baking pan.

4 Bake for 25 to 30 minutes, until lightly colored on top. Cool in the pan on a wire rack before cutting into large or small bars.

Baking notes: You can substitute lemon or orange juice and zest for the grapefruit ingredients. An orange or lemon icing would go very well with these bars.

GUMDROP BARS

Bar Cookies

YIELD: *2 to 3 dozen*
TOTAL TIME: *35 minutes*

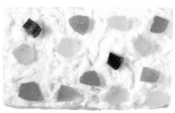

2 cups all-purpose flour
1 teaspoon ground cinnamon
¼ teaspoon salt
3 large eggs
2 cups packed light brown sugar
¼ cup evaporated milk
1 cup walnuts, chopped fine
1 cup gumdrops, chopped

1 Preheat the oven to 325 degrees. Lightly grease a 9-inch square baking pan.

2 Combine the flour, cinnamon, and salt.

3 In a large bowl, beat the eggs until thick and light-colored. Beat in the brown sugar. Beat in the milk. Gradually blend in the dry ingredients. Stir in the walnuts and gumdrops. Spread the dough evenly in the prepared baking pan.

4 Bake for 30 to 35 minutes, until lightly colored on top. Transfer to wire racks to cool.

Baking notes: For a whimsical look, frost the bars with Vanilla Icing and decorate with sliced gumdrops.

Hazelnut Bars

Bar Cookies

YIELD: *1 to 2 dozen*
TOTAL TIME: *30 minutes*

¾ cup all-purpose flour
½ cup hazelnuts, ground
⅛ teaspoon baking powder
⅛ teaspoon ground cinnamon
⅛ teaspoon ground nutmeg
⅛ teaspoon ground cloves
¼ teaspoon salt
6 tablespoons vegetable shortening
½ cup powdered sugar
1 teaspoon grated lemon zest

1 Preheat the oven to 375 degrees.

2 Combine the flour, hazelnuts, baking powder, spices, and salt.

3 In a large bowl, cream the vegetable shortening and powdered sugar. Beat in the lemon zest. Gradually blend in the dry ingredients. Press the dough evenly into an ungreased 9-inch square baking pan.

4 Bake for 18 to 20 minutes, until the top is golden and firm to the touch. Cool in the pan on a wire rack before cutting into large or small bars.

Hazelnut Squares

Bar Cookies

YIELD: *1 to 2 dozen*
TOTAL TIME: *50 minutes*

CRUST
1 cup all-purpose flour
¼ teaspoon salt
¼ cup vegetable shortening

TOPPING
2 tablespoons all-purpose flour
¼ teaspoon salt
2 large eggs
¾ cup granulated sugar
1 teaspoon rum
2 cups flaked coconut
1 cup hazelnuts, chopped

1 Preheat the oven to 350 degrees. Lightly grease a 9-inch square baking pan.

2 To make the crust, combine the flour and salt in a medium bowl. Cut in the vegetable shortening until the mixture resembles coarse crumbs. Press evenly into the prepared baking pan.

3 Bake for 15 minutes.

4 Meanwhile, make the topping: Combine the flour and salt.

5 In a medium bowl, beat the eggs and sugar until thick. Beat in the rum. Gradually blend in the dry ingredients. Stir in the coconut and hazelnuts.

6 Spread the topping over the top of the hot crust. Bake for 15 minutes longer, or until firm to the touch. Cool in the pan on a wire rack before cutting into large or small bars.

Health Bars

Bar Cookies

Yield: *2 to 3 dozen*
Total time: *35 minutes*

½ cup all-purpose flour
¼ cup whole wheat flour
½ cup wheat germ
1 teaspoon baking powder
½ cup vegetable shortening
2 ounces carob squares
1¼ cups honey
2 large eggs
1 teaspoon vanilla extract
½ cup pecans, chopped

1 Preheat the oven to 350 degrees. Lightly grease a 13 by 9-inch baking pan.

2 Combine the two flours, the wheat germ, and baking powder.

3 In a large saucepan, melt the vegetable shortening and carob with the honey, stirring until smooth. Remove from the heat and beat in the eggs one at a time. Beat in the vanilla extract. Gradually blend in the dry ingredients. Stir in the pecans. Spread the dough evenly in the prepared baking pan.

4 Bake for 25 to 30 minutes, until lightly colored on top and firm to the touch. Cool in the pan on a wire rack before cutting into large or small bars.

5 Wrap the bars individually in waxed paper to store.

Hello Dolly Cookies

Bar Cookies

Yield: *1 to 2 dozen*
Total time: *35 minutes*

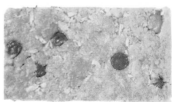

1 cup graham cracker crumbs
1 cup (6 ounces) semisweet chocolate chips
1 cup walnuts, chopped
1 cup shredded coconut
¼ cup butter, melted
One 14-ounce can sweetened condensed milk

1 Preheat the oven to 350 degrees. Lightly grease a 9-inch square baking pan.

2 Combine the graham crackers, chocolate chips, walnuts, and coconut in a medium bowl.

3 Pour the melted butter over the dry ingredients and stir. Press the mixture evenly into the prepared baking pan. Drizzle the condensed milk over the top.

4 Bake for 25 to 30 minutes, until lightly colored on top. Cool in the pan on a wire rack before cutting into large or small bars.

Baking notes: Other cookies, such as chocolate or vanilla wafers, can be substituted for graham cracker.

HELEN'S CHEESECAKE BARS

Bar Cookies

YIELD: *1 to 3 dozen*
TOTAL TIME: *45 minutes*

CRUST

2 cups (12 ounces) white chocolate chips
6 tablespoons butter, at room temperature
2 cups graham cracker crumbs
2 cups almonds, chopped

FILLING

1 pound cream cheese, at room temperature
½ cup granulated sugar
4 large eggs
1 tablespoon fresh lemon juice
1 tablespoon Amaretto
¼ cup all-purpose flour

1 Preheat the oven to 350 degrees. Lightly grease a 15 by 10-inch baking pan.

2 To make the crust, melt the chocolate chips and butter in a double boiler, stirring until smooth. Remove from the heat and blend in the graham cracker crumbs and almonds. Reserve 1½ cups of the mixture for topping, and press the remaining mixture evenly into the prepared baking pan.

3 Bake for 12 minutes.

4 Meanwhile, make the filling: In a medium bowl, beat the cream cheese and sugar. Beat in the eggs, lemon juice, and Amaretto. Beat in the flour.

5 Pour the filling over the hot crust. Sprinkle the reserved crust mixture over the top.

6 Bake for 20 to 25 minutes longer, until lightly colored on top and firm to the touch. Cool in the pan on a wire rack before cutting into large or small bars.

Baking notes: Slivered or chopped almonds may be added to the topping mixture.

HIKER'S TREATS

Bar Cookies

YIELD: *1 to 2 dozen*
TOTAL TIME: *45 minutes*

¾ cup all-purpose flour
½ cup rolled oats
¼ cup toasted wheat germ
6 tablespoons packed light brown
sugar
1 tablespoon grated orange zest
½ cup vegetable shortening

TOPPING
2 large eggs
6 tablespoon packed light brown
sugar
½ cup shredded coconut
⅔ cup slivered almonds

1 Preheat the oven to 350
degrees. Lightly grease an 8-inch
square baking pan.

2 Combine the flour, oats, wheat
germ, brown sugar, and orange
zest in a bowl. Cut in the vegetable shortening until the mixture resembles coarse crumbs.
Press the dough, evenly into the
prepared baking pan.

3 To make the topping, in a
medium bowl, beat the eggs with
the brown sugar until thick. Stir
in the coconut. Pour over the
dough and sprinkle the almonds
over the top.

4 Bake for 30 to 35 minutes, until
lighly colored on top and firm to
the touch. Cool in the pan on
wire rack before cutting into
large or small bars.

Baking notes: To enhance the
flavor of these bars, add ¼ teaspoon almond extract to the topping. Raisins may be added to
the dough.

HONEY BROWNIES

Bar Cookies

YIELD: *2 dozen*
TOTAL TIME: *35 minutes*

¾ cup all-purpose flour
2 tablespoons unsweetened cocoa
powder
¾ teaspoon baking powder
¼ teaspoon salt
⅓ cup plus 2 tablespoons vegetable
shortening
¾ cup honey
2 large eggs

1 Preheat the oven to 325
degrees. Lightly grease an 8-inch
square baking pan.

2 Combine the flour, cocoa powder, baking powder, and salt.

3 In a saucepan, melt the vegetable shortening with the honey.
Remove from the heat and beat
in the eggs one at a time. Gradually blend in the dry ingredients.
Spread the batter evenly into the
prepared baking pan.

4 Bake for 25 to 30 minutes, or
until a toothpick inserted in the
center comes out clean. Cool in
the pan on a wire rack before cutting into large or small bars.

Honey Date Bars

Bar Cookies

YIELD: *1 to 3 dozen*
TOTAL TIME: *40 minutes*

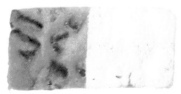

¾ cup all-purpose flour
¾ teaspoon baking powder
¼ teaspoon salt
3 tablespoons vegetable shortening
¾ cup honey
2 large eggs
1 cup dates, pitted and chopped
⅔ cup walnuts, chopped fine
Powdered sugar for coating

1 Preheat the oven to 350 degrees. Lightly grease a 9-inch square baking pan.

2 Combine the flour, baking powder, and salt.

3 In a large saucepan, melt the vegetable shortening with the honey, stirring until smooth. Remove from the heat and beat in the eggs one at a time. Gradually blend in the dry ingredients. Stir in the dates and walnuts. Spread the mixture evenly in the prepared baking pan.

4 Bake for 25 to 30 minutes, until lightly colored on top. Cool in the pan on a wire rack.

5 Cut into large or small bars, and dip half of each bar in powdered sugar.

Honey Raisin Bars

Bar Cookie

YIELD: *2 to 3 dozen*
TOTAL TIME: *35 minutes*

1½ cups all-purpose flour
1½ teaspoons baking powder
¼ teaspoon baking soda
¼ teaspoon salt
½ cup granulated sugar
½ cup honey
¼ cup butter, at room temperature
1 large egg
½ cup milk
1½ cups cornflakes, crushed
1 cup golden raisins

1 Preheat the oven to 350 degees. Lightly grease a 15 by 10-inch baking pan.

2 Combine the flour, baking powder, baking soda, and salt.

3 In a large bowl, beat the sugar, honey, and butter together until smooth. Beat in the egg. Beat in the milk. Gradually blend in the dry ingredients. Fold in the cornflakes and raisins. Spread the dough evenly in the prepared baking pan.

4 Bake for 15 to 20 minutes, until lightly colored on top. Cool in the pan on a wire rack before cutting into large or small bars.

ITALIAN ALMOND COOKIES

Bar Cookies
YIELD: *1 to 3 dozen*
TOTAL TIME: *75 minutes*

2⅔ cups all-purpose flour
1 cup almonds, ground
Pinch of salt
1 cup vegetable shortening
1 cup granulated sugar
2 tablespoons fresh lemon juice
1 tablespoon brandy
1 teaspoon grated lemon zest

1 Preheat the oven to 350 degrees. Lightly grease a 9-inch square baking pan.
2 Combine the flour, almonds, and salt.
3 In a large bowl, cream the vegetable shortening and sugar. Beat in the lemon juice and brandy. Beat in the lemon zest. Gradually blend in the dry ingredients. Spread the mixture evenly in the prepared baking pan. (Do not press down on the mixture.)
4 Bake for 50 to 60 minutes, until lightly colored on top. Cool in the pan on a wire rack before cutting into large or small bars.

JAM-FILLED STRIPS

Bar Cookies
(Microwave Recipe)
YIELD:: *1 to 2 dozen*
TOTAL TIME: *30 minutes*
CHILLING TIME: *1 hour*

1½ cups all-purpose flour
2 tablespoons granulated sugar
½ teaspoon salt
½ cup butter
1 large egg
1 cup apricot preserves

1 In a large bowl, combine the flour, sugar, and salt. Cut in the butter. Add the egg and stir to form a soft dough. Divide the dough in half. Wrap in waxed paper and chill for 1 hour.
2 On a floured surface, roll out one-half of the dough to a 12 by 6-inch rectangle. Trim the edges and place the dough on a microwave-safe baking sheet. Spread the apricot preserves evenly over the dough. Roll out the remaining dough to a rectangle and place on top of the preserves.
3 Bake on high for 3 minutes. Cool on the baking sheet on a wire rack before cutting into large or small bars.

Jam Squares

Bar Cookies

YIELD: *1 to 3 dozen*
TOTAL TIME: *50 minutes*

CRUST
1½ cups all-purpose flour
¼ teaspoon salt
½ cup butter
2 to 2½ tablespoons ice water

TOPPING
2 each large eggs
½ cup powdered sugar
2½ cups flaked coconut
⅓ cup raspberry preserves

1 Preheat the oven to 400 degrees.

2 To make the crust, combine the flour and salt in a medium bowl. Cut in the butter until the mixture resembles coarse crumbs. Add just enough water to make a soft dough. Press the dough evenly into an ungreased 9-inch square baking pan.

3 Bake for 20 minutes.

4 Meanwhile, make the topping: In a medium bowl, beat the eggs until thick and light-colored. Beat in the powdered sugar. Stir in the coconut.

5 Spread the raspberry preserves over the hot crust. Spread the topping over the preserves.

6 Bake for 20 to 25 minutes longer, until lightly colored on top and firm to the touch. Cool in the pan on a wire rack before cutting into large or small bars.

Jan Hagel

Bar Cookies

YIELD: *1 to 3 dozen*
TOTAL TIME: *30 minutes*

CRUST
2 cups all-purpose flour
¼ teaspoon salt
1 cup vegetable shortening
1 cup packed light brown sugar
1 large egg yolk

TOPPING
1 large egg white
1 cup granulated sugar
½ teaspoon ground cinnamon
½ cup walnuts, chopped

1 Preheat the oven to 375 degrees. Lightly grease a 9-inch square baking pan.

2 To make the crust, combine the flour and salt.

3 In a large bowl, cream the vegetable shortening and brown sugar. Beat in the egg yolk. Gradually blend in the dry ingredients. Spread the dough evenly in the prepared baking pan.

4 To make the topping, in a medium bowl, beat the egg white until stiff but not dry. Gradually fold in the sugar and cinnamon. Fold in the nuts. Spread the topping over the dough.

5 Bake for 18 to 20 minutes, until lightly colored on top and firm to the touch. Cool in the pan on a wire rack before cutting into large or small bars.

Jewel Bars

Bar Cookies

YIELD: *1 to 2 dozen*
TOTAL TIME: *45 minutes*

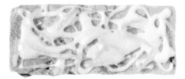

2¼ cups all-purpose flour
1½ teaspoons baking powder
1 teaspoon ground cinnamon
1 teaspoon ground nutmeg
1 teaspoon salt
½ cup vegetable shortening
1½ cups packed light brown sugar
8 ounces cream cheese, at room
  temperature
1 large egg
¼ cup honey
1 cup walnuts, chopped
1 cup mixed candied fruit, chopped
  fine
1 cup raisins
Lemon Icing (see Pantry)

1 Preheat the oven to 350
degrees. Lightly grease a 9-inch
square baking pan.

2 Combine the flour, baking
powder, cinnamon, nutmeg, and
salt.

3 In a large bowl, cream the vegetable shortening and sugar. Beat
in the cream cheese. Beat in the
egg and honey. Gradually blend
in the dry ingredients. Stir in the
walnuts, mixed fruit, and raisins.
Spread the mixture evenly in the
prepared baking pan.

4 Bake for 30 to 35 minutes, until
a toothpick inserted in the center
comes out clean. Cool in the pan
on a wire rack.

5 Spread the icing over the
cooled cookies and cut into large
or small bars.

Baking notes: If you prefer, use
just one kind of candied fruit,
such as cherries.

Kentucky Pecan Bars

Bar Cookies

YIELD: *1 to 2 dozen*
TOTAL TIME: *45 minutes*

CRUST
1⅓ cups all-purpose flour
1¼ cups packed light brown sugar
½ teaspoon baking soda
½ teaspoon salt
1 cup pecans, toasted and chopped
½ cup vegetable shortening

TOPPING
3 large eggs
⅓ cup granulated sugar
¼ cup butter, at room temperature
3 tablespoons bourbon
1 teaspoon vanilla extract

1 Preheat the oven to 350
degrees. Lightly grease an 8-inch
square baking pan.

2 To make the crust, combine the
flour, brown sugar, baking soda,
salt, and pecans. Cut in the vegetable shortening until the mixture resembles coarse crumbs.
Press the mixture evenly into the
prepared baking pans.

3 Bake for 15 minutes.

4 Meanwhile, make the topping:
In a medium bowl, beat the eggs
until thick and light-colored. Beat
in the sugar and butter. Beat in
the bourbon and vanilla extract.

5 Spread the topping over the
hot crust. Bake for 20 to 25 minutes longer, until lightly colored
and firm to the touch. Cool in the
pan on a wire rack before cutting
into large or small bars.

Baking notes: You can decorate
these bars by arranging pecan
halves on the topping before
baking.

KRISPIES

Bar Cookies

YIELD: *1 to 2 dozen*
TOTAL TIME: *30 minutes*

1½ ounces milk chocolate
½ cup butter
½ cup corn syrup
1 cup powdered sugar
2 teaspoons vanilla extract
4 cups rice krispies

1 Lightly grease a 13 by 9-inch baking pan. Chill in the freezer.

2 In a large saucepan, melt the chocolate and butter with the corn syrup, stirring until smooth. Remove from the heat and beat in the powdered sugar. Beat in the vanilla extract. Stir in the rice krispies. Press the mixture evenly into the prepared baking pan.

3 Chill in the refrigerator for 20 minutes or until set. Cut into large or small bars.

LEMON BARS I

Bar Cookies

YIELD: *2 to 3 dozen*
TOTAL TIME: *40 minutes*

2½ cups all-purpose flour
2 teaspoons baking powder
1 teaspoon baking soda
½ teaspoon ground allspice
¼ cup vegetable shortening
2 large eggs
1½ cups frozen lemon juice concentrate, thawed
1 teaspoon lemon extract
1 cup golden raisins
1 cup walnuts, chopped
¾ cup flaked coconut
¾ cup canned crushed pineapple, drained

1 Preheat the oven to 350 degrees. Lightly grease a 13 by 9-inch baking pan.

2 Combine the flour, baking powder, baking soda, and allspice.

3 In a large bowl, cream the vegetable shortening until light and fluffy. Beat in the eggs. Beat in the lemon juice concentrate and lemon extract. Gradually blend in the dry ingredients. Fold in the raisins and walnuts. Spread the mixture evenly in the prepared baking pan. Sprinkle the coconut and pineapple over the top.

4 Bake for 20 to 25 minutes, until lightly colored on top and firm to the touch. Cool in the pan on a wire rack before cutting into large or small bars.

LEMON BARS II

Bar Cookies

YIELD: *1 to 3 dozen*
TOTAL TIME: *40 minutes*

2 cups all-purpose flour
1 teaspoon baking soda
1 teaspoon ground cinnamon
½ teaspoon ground nutmeg
½ teaspoon salt
¾ cup vegetable shortening
1½ cups packed light brown sugar
2 large eggs
3 tablespoons fresh lemon juice
3 tablespoons grated lemon zest
1 cup raisins

1 Preheat the oven to 350 degrees. Lightly grease a 9-inch square baking pan.

2 Combine the flour, baking soda, spices, and salt.

3 In a large bowl, cream the vegetable shortening and brown sugar. Beat in the eggs one at a time. Beat in the lemon juice and zest. Stir in the raisins. Spread the dough evenly in the prepared baking pan.

4 Bake for 25 to 30 minutes, until lightly colored on top. Cool in the pan on a wire rack before cutting into large or small bars.

LEMON BARS III

Bar Cookies

YIELD: *1 to 3 dozen*
TOTAL TIME: *55 minutes*

CRUST
2 cups all-purpose flour
½ cup powdered sugar
1 cup vegetable shortening

TOPPING
4 large eggs
2 cups granulated sugar
⅓ cup fresh lemon juice
¼ cup all-purpose flour
½ teaspoon baking powder

1 Preheat the oven to 350 degrees. Lightly grease a 13 by 9 inch baking pan.

2 To make the crust, combine the flour and powdered sugar in a medium bowl. Cut in the vegetable shortening until the mixture resembles coarse crumbs. Press the mixture evenly into the prepared baking pan.

3 Bake for 20 minutes.

4 Meanwhile make the topping: In a large bowl, beat the eggs until thick and light-colored. Beat in the sugar. Beat in the lemon juice. Beat in the flour and baking powder.

5 Pour the topping over the hot crust. Bake for 20 to 25 minutes longer, until lightly colored on top and firm to the touch. Cool in the pan on a wire rack before cutting into large or small bars.

LEMON-GLAZED APPLE SQUARES

Bar Cookies

YIELD: *2 to 3 dozen*
TOTAL TIME: *70 minutes*

CRUST
2 cups all-purpose flour
¼ cup granulated sugar
¾ cup vegetable shortening
2 large egg yolks

FILLING
1½ cups granola cereal
½ cup almonds, chopped fine
½ cup granulated sugar
1 teaspoon ground cinnamon
3 tablespoons fresh lemon juice
6 medium apples, peeled, cored, and sliced

GLAZE
¾ cup powdered sugar
2 tablespoons fresh lemon juice

1 Preheat the oven to 350 degrees. Lightly grease a 15 by 10-inch baking pan.

2 To make the crust, combine the flour and sugar in a large bowl. Cut in the vegetable shortening until the mixture resembles coarse crumbs. Work in the egg yolks one at a time until a smooth dough forms. Press the dough evenly into the prepared baking pan.

3 Combine the granola, almonds, sugar, and cinnamon. Stir in the lemon juice.

4 Layer the sliced apples on top of the crust. Sprinkle the granola mixture over the apples.

5 Bake for 55 to 60 minutes, until the top is lightly colored and the apples are soft.

6 Meanwhile, make the glaze: Combine the powdered sugar and lemon juice in a small bowl and stir until smooth.

7 Drizzle the glaze over the top of the warm bars. Cool in the pan on a wire rack before cutting into large or small bars.

MACADAMIA NUT BARS

Bar Cookies

YIELD: *1 to 3 dozen*
TOTAL TIME: *55 minutes*

CRUST
2 cups all-purpose flour
2 cups packed light brown sugar
1 cup vegetable shortening

FILLING
1 large egg
1 teaspoon baking soda
1 cup sour cream
1 cup macadamia nuts, chopped

1 Preheat the oven to 350 degrees. Lightly grease a 13 by 9-inch baking pan.

2 To make the crust, combine the flour and brown sugar in a large bowl. Cut in the vegetable shortening until the mixture resembles coarse crumbs. Press evenly into the prepared baking pan.

3 To prepare the filling, in a medium bowl, beat the egg until thick and light-colored. Beat in the baking soda. Beat in the sour cream. Pour the filling over the crust. Sprinkle the chopped macadamia nuts over the top.

4 Bake for 45 to 50 minutes, or until firm to the touch. Cool in the pan on a wire rack before cutting into large or small bars.

MAGIC BARS

Bar Cookies

YIELD: *1 to 3 dozen*
TOTAL TIME: *45 minutes*

1½ cups graham cracker crumbs
½ cup butter, melted
1 cup flaked coconut
1 cup (6 ounces) butterscotch chips
1 cup pecans, chopped

1 Preheat the oven to 350 degrees. Lightly grease a 13 by 9-inch baking pan.

2 Put the graham cracker crumbs in a large bowl and stir in the butter. Press the mixture into the prepared baking pan.

3 Combine the coconut, butterscotch chips, and pecans in a medium bowl and toss to mix. Spread this mixture evenly over the graham cracker mixture.

4 Bake for 25 to 30 minutes, until lightly colored on top. Cool in the pan on a wire rack before cutting into large or small bars.

Marbled Cream Cheese Brownies

Bar Cookies

Yield: 1 to 3 dozen
Total time: 45 minutes

4 ounces cream cheese, at room
   temperature
5 tablespoons vegetable shortening
1 cup granulated sugar
1 tablespoon cornstarch
3 large eggs
1½ teaspoons vanilla extract
½ teaspoon fresh lemon juice
½ cup all-purpose flour
½ teaspoon baking powder
½ teaspoon salt
⅔ cup semisweet chocolate chips

1 Preheat the oven to 350
degrees. Lightly grease a 9-inch
square baking pan.

2 In a medium bowl, combine
the cream cheese, 2 tablespoons
of the vegetable shortening, ¼
cup of the sugar, and the cornstarch and beat until smooth.
Beat in 1 of the eggs. Beat in the
½ teaspoon of the vanilla extract
and lemon juice. Set aside.

3 Combine the flour, baking
powder, and salt.

4 In the top of a double boiler,
melt the chocolate and the
remaining 3 tablespoons vegetable shortening, stirring until
smooth. Remove from the heat
and stir in the remaining 1 teaspoon vanilla extract.

5 In a large bowl, beat the
remaining 2 eggs and ¾ cup
sugar. Beat in the cooled chocolate. Beat in the dry ingredients.

6 Spread the batter evenly in the
prepared baking pan. Pour the
cream cheese mixture over the
top and swirl a knife back and
forth a few times through the
mixture to marble it.

7 Bake for 25 to 30 minutes, until
a toothpick inserted in the center
comes out clean. Cool in the pan
on a wire rack before cutting into
large or small bars.

Meringue-Topped Brownies

Bar Cookies

YIELD: *1 to 3 dozen*
TOTAL TIME: *45 minutes*

2 cups all-purpose flour
1 teaspoon baking powder
¼ teaspoon baking soda
¼ teaspoon salt
¼ cup vegetable shortening
¼ cup butter, at room temperature
½ cup granulated sugar
½ cup packed light brown sugar
2 large egg yolks
1 tablespoon strong brewed coffee
1½ teaspoons crème de cacao
1½ cups (9 ounces) semisweet
  chocolate chips

TOPPING
2 large egg whites
1 cup granulated sugar

1 Preheat the oven to 375 degrees. Lightly grease a 13 by 9-inch baking pan.

2 Combine the flour, baking powder, baking soda, and salt.

3 In a large bowl, cream the vegetable shortening, butter, and two sugars. Beat in the egg yolks. Beat in the coffee and crème de cacao. Gradually blend in the dry ingredients.

4 Spread the batter evenly in the prepared baking pan. Sprinkle the chocolate chips over the top.

5 To make the topping, in a bowl, beat the egg whites until foamy. Gradually beat in the sugar and beat until the whites form stiff peaks. Spread the topping over the chocolate chips.

6 Bake for 20 to 25 minutes, until lightly colored and firm to the touch. Cool in the pan on a wire rack before cutting into large or small bars.

Mint Brownies

Bar Cookies

YIELD: *1 to 2 dozen*
TOTAL TIME: *35 minutes*

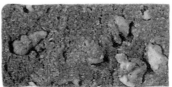

½ cup vegetable shortening
3 ounces bittersweet chocolate,
  chopped
2 cups granulated sugar
4 large egg yolks
½ teaspoon vanilla extract
⅛ teaspoon mint extract
1 cup all-purpose flour
1 cup walnuts, chopped

1 Preheat the oven to 325 degrees. Lightly grease a 9-inch square baking pan.

2 In the top of a double boiler, melt the vegetable shortening and chocolate, stirring until smooth. Remove from the heat and stir in the sugar. Beat in the egg yolks. Beat in the vanilla and mint extracts. Gradually blend in the flour. Stir in the walnuts. Spread the mixture evenly in the prepared baking pan.

3 Bake for 25 to 35 minutes, or until a toothpick inserted in the center comes out clean. Cool in the pan on a wire rack before cutting into large or small bars.

Mint Bars

Bar Cookies

YIELD: *1 to 3 dozen*
TOTAL TIME: *35 minutes*
CHILLING TIME: *2 hours*

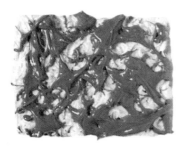

1 cup all-purpose flour
½ teaspoon baking powder
½ cup vegetable shortening
1 cup granulated sugar
4 large eggs
2 cups chocolate syrup

TOPPING
½ cup margarine
2 cups powdered sugar
2 tablespoons fresh milk
1 teaspoon crème de menthe
3 drops green food coloring
6 ounces (1 cup) semisweet chocolate chips
½ cup butter

1 Preheat the oven to 350 degrees. Lightly grease a 13 by 9-inch baking pan.

2 Combine the flour and baking powder.

3 In a large bowl, cream the vegetable shortening and sugar. Beat in the eggs. Beat in the chocolate syrup. Gradually blend in the dry ingredients. Spread the dough evenly in the prepared baking pan.

4 Bake for 20 to 25 minutes, until the top is lightly colored. Let cool in the pan on a wire rack, then refrigerate for 1 hour or until chilled.

5 To make the topping, cream the butter and powdered sugar in a large bowl. Beat in the milk and crème de menthe. Beat in the food coloring. Spread evenly over the chilled bars. Chill for 1 hour longer.

6 In the top of a double boiler, melt the chocolate chips and butter, stirring until smooth. Carefully spread this mixture over the chilled cookies and cut into large or small bars.

Mocha-Coffee Brownies

Bar Cookies
YIELD: *1 to 2 dozen*
TOTAL TIME: *35 minutes*

2 ounces semisweet chocolate, chopped
⅓ cup vegetable shortening
¾ cup all-purpose flour
½ teaspoon baking powder
¼ teaspoon salt
2 large eggs
1 cup granulated sugar
1 teaspoon vanilla extract
2½ tablespoons instant mocha coffee crystals
½ cup walnuts, chopped

1 Preheat the oven to 375 degrees. Lightly grease an 8-inch square baking pan.

2 In a double boiler, melt the chocolate and vegetable shortening, stirring until smooth. Remove from the heat.

3 Combine the flour, baking powder, and salt.

4 In a large bowl, beat the eggs until thick and light-colored. Beat in the sugar. Beat in the melted chocolate mixture and vanilla extract. Gradually blend in the dry ingredients. Stir in the coffee crystals. Spread the mixture evenly in the prepared baking pan. Sprinkle the walnuts on top.

5 Bake for 20 to 25 minutes, until a toothpick inserted into the center comes out clean. Cool in the pan on a wire rack before cutting into large or small bars.

No-Bake Oatmeal Bars

Bar Cookies
YIELD: *2 to 3 dozen*
TOTAL TIME: *20 minutes*

3 tablespoons vegetable shortening
3 cups miniature marshmallows
¼ cup honey
½ cup peanut butter
1 cup raisins
¼ cup rolled oats
½ cup peanuts, chopped

1 Lightly grease a 9-inch square baking pan.

2 In a large saucepan, combine the vegetable shortening, marshmallows, honey, and peanut butter and heat, stirring, until smooth. Remove from the heat and gradually blend in the raisins, oats, and peanuts.

3 Spread the mixture evenly in the prepared baking pan. Chill for at least 2 hours.

4 Cut into large or small bars and wrap individually in waxed paper.

Baking notes: You can spread this mixture in a larger pan to make make thinner bars. For a different version, plump the raisins in boiling water while heating the marshmallow mixture. Spread half of the mixture in the prepared pan. Drain the raisins, pat dry, and sprinkle over the marshmallow mixture. Then sprinkle with finely chopped peanuts, and spread the remaining marshmallow mixture on top.

Nut Bars I

Bar Cookies

YIELD: *3 to 4 dozen*
TOTAL TIME: *25 minutes*

3 large egg whites
1 cup sweetened condensed milk
1 teaspoon vanilla extract
1 teaspoon almond extract
4 cups shredded coconut
1 cup walnuts, ground fine
1 cup dates, pitted and chopped

1 Preheat the oven to 350 degrees. Lightly grease a 9-inch square baking pan.
2 In a large bowl, beat the egg whites until foamy. Beat in the milk and vanilla and almond extracts. Gradually blend in the coconut, walnuts, and dates. Spread the mixture evenly in the prepared baking pan.
3 Bake for 10 to 12 minutes, until lightly colored on top. Cool in the pan on a wire rack before cutting into large or small bars.

Baking notes: To make sandwich cookies using this recipe, spread the batter in a 13 by 9-inch baking pan and bake. Cut into bars and fill with a custard or cream filling. This same recipe can be used for drop cookies; drop onto well-greased baking sheets.

Nut Bars II

Bar Cookies

YIELD: *1 to 2 dozen*
TOTAL TIME: *45 minutes*

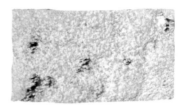

½ cup all-purpose flour
1 cup walnuts, ground fine
½ teaspoons baking powder
½ teaspoon salt
½ cup granulated sugar
2 large eggs
½ teaspoon vanilla extract
1 cup prunes, pitted and chopped
Powdered sugar for sprinkling

1 Preheat the oven to 325 degrees. Lightly grease an 8-inch square baking pan.
2 Combine the flour, walnuts, baking powder, and salt.
3 In a large bowl, beat the sugar and eggs until thick and light-colored. Beat in the vanilla extract. Gradually blend in the dry ingredients. Stir in the prunes. Spread the mixture evenly in the prepared baking pan.
4 Bake for 35 to 40 minutes, until a toothpick inserted into the center comes out clean. Cool slightly in the pan, then cut into large or small bars. Sprinkle the warm bars with powdered sugar before removing from the pan.

OATMEAL BROWNIES

Bar Cookies

YIELD: *1 to 2 dozen*
TOTAL TIME: *35 minutes*

3 ounces semisweet chocolate, chopped
1 cup all-purpose flour
½ teaspoon salt
⅔ cup vegetable shortening
1 cup packed light brown sugar
½ cup granulated sugar
4 large eggs
2 teaspoons vanilla extract
1 cup rolled oats
1 cup walnuts, chopped

1 Preheat the oven to 325 degrees. Lightly grease a 13 by 9-inch baking pan.

2 Melt the chocolate in a double boiler over low heat, stirring until smooth. Remove from the heat.

3 Combine the flour and salt.

4 In a large bowl, cream the vegetable shortening and two sugars. Beat in the eggs one at a time, beating well after each addition. Beat in the vanilla extract. Beat in the melted chocolate. Gradually blend in the dry ingredients. Fold in the oats and walnuts. Spread the mixture evenly in the prepared baking pan.

5 Bake for 25 to 30 minutes, or until a toothpick inserted in the center comes out clean; don't overbake. Cool in the pan on a wire rack before cutting into large or small bars.

Baking notes: Raisins can be added to this batter.

OATMEAL LEMONADE BARS

Bar Cookies

YIELD: *1 to 2 dozen*
TOTAL TIME: *50 minutes*

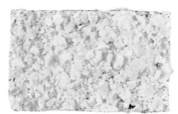

FILLING
12 ounces prunes, pitted
¾ cup water
¾ cup frozen lemon juice concentrate, thawed
⅓ cup granulated sugar
¼ cup all-purpose flour
¼ teaspoon salt

CRUST
1 cup all-purpose flour
1 cup rolled oats
¼ teaspoon baking soda
½ cup vegetable shortening
1 cup packed light brown sugar

1 Preheat the oven to 400 degrees. Lightly grease a 13 by 9-inch baking pan.

2 To make the filling, combine the prunes, water and lemon juice concentrate in a saucepan and bring to a boil. Cook for 15 minutes, or until the prunes are a puree. Remove from the heat and stir in the sugar, flour, and salt.

3 To make the crust, combine the flour, oats, and baking soda.

4 In a large bowl, cream the vegetable shortening and brown sugar. Gradually blend in the dry ingredients.

5 Spread half of the crust mixture evenly in the bottom of the prepared baking pan. Spread the filling over the crust, leaving a ½-inch border all around. Spread the remaining crust mixture over the filling and press down lightly.

6 Bake for 18 to 20 minutes, until golden brown on top. Cool in the pan on a wire rack before cutting into large or small bars.

Orange Bars I

Bar Cookies

YIELD: *2 to 3 dozen*
TOTAL TIME: *35 minutes*

2½ cups all-purpose flour
2 teaspoons baking powder
1 teaspoon baking soda
1 teaspoon ground cardamom
2 large eggs
¼ cup vegetable shortening, melted
1½ cups frozen orange juice concentrate, thawed
1 teaspoon orange liqueur
1 cup cranberries, chopped
1 cup almonds, chopped
¾ cup shredded coconut

1 Preheat the oven to 350 degrees. Lightly grease a 13 by 9-inch baking pan.

2 Combine the flour, baking powder, baking soda, and cardamom.

3 In a large bowl, beat together the eggs, vegetable shortening, orange juice concentrate, and orange liqueur until smooth. Gradually blend in the dry ingredients. Stir in the cranberries and almonds. Spread the mixture evenly in the prepared baking pan and sprinkle the coconut over the top.

4 Bake for 20 to 25 minutes, until the top is lightly colored. Cool in the pan on a wire rack before cutting into large or small bars.

Orange Bars II

Bar Cookies

YIELD: *1 to 3 dozen*
TOTAL TIME: *35 minutes*

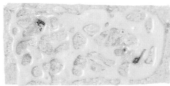

2 cups all-purpose flour
1 teaspoon baking soda
1 teaspoon ground cinnamon
½ teaspoon ground cloves
½ teaspoon salt
¾ cup vegetable shortening
1½ cups packed light brown sugar
2 large eggs
3 tablespoons fresh orange juice
3 tablespoons grated orange zest
1 cup raisins
1 cup walnuts, chopped

1 Preheat the oven to 350 degrees. Lightly grease a 9-inch square baking pan.

2 Combine the flour, baking soda, spices, and salt.

3 In a large bowl, cream the vegetable shortening and brown sugar. Beat in the eggs. Beat in the orange juice and zest. Gradually blend in the dry ingredients. Fold in the raisins and walnuts. Spread the mixture evenly in the prepared baking pan.

4 Bake for 25 to 30 minutes, until lightly colored on top. Cool in the pan on a wire rack before cutting into large or small bars.

Baking notes: Frost if desired when cooled; orange or lemon icing is good with these bars.

ORANGE BARS III

Bar Cookies

YIELD: *1 to 3 dozen*
TOTAL TIME: *60 minutes*

CRUST
2 cups all-purpose flour
¼ cup walnuts, ground fine
½ cup vegetable shortening
¼ cup granulated sugar

TOPPING
¼ cup all-purpose flour
¼ cup rolled oats
½ teaspoon baking powder
2 cups granulated sugar
4 large eggs
¼ cup fresh orange juice

1 Preheat the oven to 350 degrees. Lightly grease a 13 by 9-inch square baking pan.

2 To make the crust, combine the flour and walnuts.

3 In a large bowl, cream together the vegetable shortening and sugar. Gradually blend in the dry ingredients. Spread the mixture evenly in the prepared baking pan.

4 Bake for 25 minutes.

5 Meanwhile, make the topping: Combine the flour, oats, and baking powder.

6 In a medium bowl, beat the sugar and eggs together until thick and light-colored. Beat in the orange juice. Gradually blend in the dry ingredients.

7 Pour the topping over the hot crust. Bake for 18 to 20 minutes longer, until the topping is lightly colored and firm to the touch. Cool in the pan on a wire rack before cutting into large or small bars.

ORANGE-CRANBERRY BARS

Bar Cookies

YIELD: *2 to 3 dozen*
TOTAL TIME: *30 minutes*

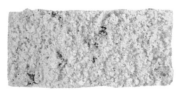

2 cups all-purpose flour
1 teaspoon baking powder
½ teaspoon baking soda
1 teaspoon ground cinnamon
¼ cup vegetable shortening
3 large eggs
⅔ cup fresh orange juice
½ teaspoon orange extract
1 cup cranberries, minced

TOPPING
⅓ cup almonds, ground fine
¼ teaspoon ground nutmeg

1 Preheat the oven to 350 degrees. Lightly grease an 8-inch square baking pan.

2 Combine the flour, baking powder, baking soda, and cinnamon.

3 In a large bowl, beat the vegetable shortening, eggs, orange juice, and orange extract until smooth. Gradually blend in the dry ingredients. Stir in the cranberries. Spread the mixture evenly in the prepared baking pan.

4 Combine the almonds and nutmeg and sprinkle over the top.

5 Bake for 20 to 25 minutes, until golden brown on top. Cool in the pan on a wire rack before cutting into large or small bars.

Peanut Blondies

Bar Cookies

Yield: *2 to 3 dozen*
Total time: *40 minutes*

½ cup vegetable shortening
2 cups packed light brown sugar
1 cup peanut butter
4 large eggs
2 teaspoons vanilla extract
1 cup all-purpose flour
2 cups peanuts, chopped

1 Preheat the oven to 350 degrees. Lightly grease a 9-inch square baking pan.

2 In a large bowl, cream the vegetable shortening and brown sugar. Beat in the peanut butter. Beat in the eggs. Beat in the vanilla extract. Gradually blend in the flour. Spread the mixture evenly in the prepared baking pan and sprinkle the chopped nuts over the top.

3 Bake for 30 to 35 minutes, until a knife inserted in the center comes out clean. Cool in the pan on a wire rack before cutting into large or small bars.

Baking notes: Chunky peanut butter makes an even nuttier bar.

Peanut Butter-Banana Squares

Bar Cookies

Yield: *2 to 3 dozen*

1 cup all-purpose flour
1 teaspoon baking powder
1 teaspoon baking soda
¼ cup peanut butter
1 cup mashed bananas
¼ cup banana-flavored yogurt
1 large egg
½ cup peanuts, chopped

1 Preheat the oven to 350 degrees. Lightly grease an 8-inch square baking pan.

2 Combine the flour, baking powder, and baking soda.

3 In a large bowl, beat the peanut butter, bananas, and yogurt until smooth. Beat in the egg. Gradually blend in the dry ingredients. Fold in the peanuts. Spread the mixture evenly in the prepared baking pan.

4 Bake for 18 to 20 minutes, until lightly colored on top and firm to the touch. Cool in the pan on a wire rack before cutting into large or small bars.

Peanut Butter Bars I

Bar Cookies

YIELD: *2 to 3 dozen*
TOTAL TIME: *40 minutes*

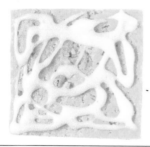

1½ cups all-purpose flour
½ teaspoon salt
2 cups packed light brown sugar
1 cup peanut butter
⅔ cup vegetable shortening
3 large eggs
1 teaspoon vanilla extract
Vanilla Icing (see Pantry)

1 Preheat the oven to 350 degrees. Lightly grease an 8-inch square baking pan.

2 Combine the flour and salt.

3 In a large bowl, beat the brown sugar, peanut butter, and vegetable shortening until smooth and creamy. Beat in the eggs. Beat in the vanilla extract. Gradually blend in the dry ingredients. Spread the mixture evenly in the prepared baking pan.

4 Bake for 30 to 35 minutes, until firm to the touch. Cool in the pan on a wire rack.

5 Drizzle the icing over the cookies and cut into large or small bars.

Peanut Butter Bars II

Bar Cookies

YIELD: *3 to 4 dozen*
TOTAL TIME: *45 minutes*

1 cup all-purpose flour
½ cup rolled oats
1 teaspoon baking powder
½ teaspoon salt
½ cup vegetable shortening
¾ cup packed light brown sugar
1 cup peanut butter
3 large eggs
½ cup milk
1 teaspoon vanilla extract
1 cup (6 ounces) semisweet chocolate chips

1 Preheat the oven to 350 degrees.

2 Combine the flour, oats, baking powder, and salt.

3 In a large bowl, cream the vegetable shortening and brown sugar. Beat in the peanut butter. Beat in the eggs. Beat in the milk and vanilla extract. Gradually blend in the dry ingredients. Spread the mixture evenly into an ungreased 8-inch square baking pan.

4 Bake for 25 to 30 minutes, until lightly colored on top. Sprinkle the chocolate chips over the hot crust. Let sit for 1 to 2 minutes to melt the chocolate, then spread it evenly over the top with a spatula. Cool in the pan on a wire rack before cutting into large or small bars.

Baking notes: Use peanut butter chips for the topping to add even more peanut butter flavor. Raisins may be added to the dough if desired.

Peanut Butter Shortbread

Bar Cookies

Yield: 3 to 4 dozen
Total time: 40 minutes

1⅓ cups all-purpose flour
1 cup rolled oats
1 cup packed light brown sugar
1 cup vegetable shortening
¼ cup peanut butter
1 large egg, separated
1 teaspoon vanilla extract
1 cup peanuts, ground fine

1 Preheat the oven to 300 degrees. Lightly grease a 15 by 10-inch baking pan.

2 Combine the flour and oats.

3 In a large bowl, beat the brown sugar, vegetable shortening, and peanut butter together until smooth and creamy. Beat in the egg yolk and vanilla extract. Gradually blend in the dry ingredients. Spread the mixture evenly in the prepared baking pan.

4 In a small bowl, beat the egg white until frothy. Spread over the dough and sprinkle the ground peanuts over the top.

5 Bake for 25 to 30 minutes, until lightly colored on top and firm to the touch. Cut into large or small bars and cool in the pan on a wire rack.

Pear Bars

Bar Cookies

Yield: 2 to 3 dozen
Total time: 40 minutes

FILLING
½ cup dates, pitted and chopped fine
1½ cups all-purpose flour
2 teaspoons baking powder
¼ teaspoon ground nutmeg
⅓ cup canola oil
2 large eggs
1½ to 2 pears, peeled, chopped and pureed
1 cup rolled oats

1 Preheat the oven to 350 degrees. Lightly grease an 8-inch square baking pan.

2 To make the filling, place the dates in a blender and process to a puree adding just enough water to reach the desired consistency.

3 Combine the flour, baking powder, and nutmeg.

4 In a large bowl, beat the oil and eggs until thick and light-colored. Beat in the pureed pears. Gradually blend in the dry ingredients. Stir in the oats.

5 Spread half of the pear mixture evenly in the bottom of the prepared baking pan. Spread the date filling on top of the batter. Spread the remaining batter over the dates.

6 Bake for 20 to 25 minutes, until lightly browned on the top. Cool in the pan on a wire rack before cutting into large or small bars.

PECAN SQUARES

Bar Cookies

YIELD: *1 to 2 dozen*
TOTAL TIME: *50 minutes*

CRUST
1 cup all-purpose flour
¼ teaspoon salt
¼ cup vegetable shortening

FILLING
2 tablespoons all-purpose flour
¼ teaspoon salt
¾ cup granulated sugar
2 large eggs
2 teaspoons bourbon
2 cups flaked coconut
1 cup pecans, chopped

1 Preheat the oven to 350 degrees. Lightly grease a 9-inch square baking pan.

2 To make the crust, combine the flour and salt in a medium bowl. Cut in the shortening until the mixture resembles coarse crumbs. Press the dough evenly into the prepared baking pan.

3 Bake for 15 minutes.

4 To make the filling, combine the flour and salt.

5 In a large bowl, beat the sugar and eggs. Beat in the bourbon. Gradually blend in the dry ingredients. Stir in the coconut and pecans.

6 Spread the filling over the hot crust. Bake for 12 to 15 minutes longer, or until lightly colored on top and firm to the touch. Cool in the pan on a wire rack before cutting into large or small bars.

PEPPARKOEK

Bar Cookies

YIELD: *3 to 4 dozen*
TOTAL TIME: *90 minutes*

4 cups all-purpose flour
1 teaspoon baking powder
1 teaspoon ground cinnamon
½ teaspoon ground cloves
1 cup packed light brown sugar
1 cup milk
1 cup molasses
1 cup candied citrus peel, chopped

1 Preheat the oven to 300 degrees. Lightly grease an 8-inch square baking pan.

2 Combine the flour, baking powder, and spices.

3 In a large bowl, beat the brown sugar, milk, and molasses until smooth. Gradually blend in the dry ingredients. Stir in the candied citrus peel. Spread the dough evenly in the prepared baking pan.

4 Bake for 1½ to 2 hours, or until lightly colored and firm to the touch. Cool in the pan on a wire rack before cutting into large or small bars.

Persimmon Bars

Bar Cookies

YIELD: *4 to 5 dozen*
TOTAL TIME: *35 minutes*

1¾ cups all-purpose flour
1 teaspoon baking soda
1 teaspoon ground nutmeg
1 teaspoon ground cinnamon
¼ teaspoon ground cloves
1 cup granulated sugar
½ cup canola oil
1 large egg
1 persimmon, peeled and pureed

1 Preheat the oven to 350 degrees. Lightly grease a 9-inch square baking pan.

2 Combine the flour, baking soda, and spices.

3 In a large bowl, beat the sugar and oil. Beat in the egg. Beat in the persimmon puree. Spread the mixture evenly in the prepared baking pan.

4 Bake for 20 to 25 minutes, until lightly colored on top and firm to the touch. Cool in the pan on a wire rack.

Pineapple-Blueberry Bars

Bar Cookies

YIELD: *2 to 3 dozen*
TOTAL TIME: *35 minutes*

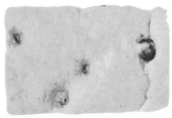

½ cup canned crushed pineapple, drained
½ cup unsweetened pineapple juice
1 teaspoon baking powder
1 teaspoon baking soda
1 teaspoon orange liqueur
1 tablespoon vegetable shortening
1 large egg
1½ cups all-purpose flour
½ cup blueberries

1 Preheat the oven to 350 degrees. Lightly grease an 8-inch square baking pan.

2 In a blender, puree the pineapple and pineapple juice.

3 Transfer pineapple puree to a large bowl and whisk in the baking powder, baking soda, orange liqueur, vegetable shortening, and the egg. Gradually blend in the flour. Fold in the blueberries. Spread the mixture evenly in the prepared baking pan.

4 Bake for 20 to 25 minutes, until lightly colored on top and firm to the touch. Cool in the pan on a wire rack before cutting into large or small bars.

Pineapple-Coconut Bars

Bar Cookies

Yield: *2 to 3 dozen*
Total time: *40 minutes*

¾ cup all-purpose flour
¾ teaspoon baking powder
½ teaspoon salt
½ cup vegetable shortening
1 cup packed light brown sugar
2 large eggs
One 8-ounce can crushed pineapple,
    drained
½ teaspoon rum
¾ cup flaked coconut

1 Preheat the oven to 350 degrees. Lightly grease a 9-inch square baking pan.

2 Combine the flour, baking powder, and salt.

3 In a large bowl, cream the vegetable shortening and brown sugar. Beat in the eggs. Beat in the pineapple and rum. Gradually blend in the dry ingredients. Stir in the coconut. Spread the mixture evenly in the prepared baking pan.

4 Bake for 25 to 30 minutes, until lightly colored on top. Cool in the pan on a wire rack before cutting into large or small bars.

Pumpkin Bars

Bar Cookies

Yield: *1 to 2 dozen*
Total time: *45 minutes*

2 cups all-purpose flour
2 teaspoons baking powder
1 teaspoon baking soda
2 teaspoons ground cinnamon
½ teaspoon ground ginger
½ teaspoon ground cloves
½ teaspoon ground nutmeg
¾ teaspoon salt
4 large eggs
2 cups granulated sugar
¾ cup vegetable oil
One 16-ounce can solid-pack
    pumpkin
Vanilla Icing (see Pantry)

1 Preheat the oven to 350 degrees. Lightly grease a 13 by 9-inch baking pan.

2 Combine the flour, baking powder, baking soda, spices, and salt.

3 In a large bowl, beat the eggs and sugar until thick and light-colored. Beat in the oil. Beat in the pumpkin. Gradually blend in the dry ingredients. Scrape the mixture into the prepared baking pan.

4 Bake for 30 to 35 minutes, until the edges pull away from the sides and the top springs back when lightly touched. Cool in the pan on a wire rack.

5 Frost the cooled cookies with the icing and cut into large or small bars.

Raisin Bars

Bar Cookies

Yield: 3 to 4 dozen
Total time: 35 minutes

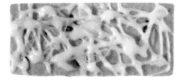

3 cups all-purpose flour
½ teaspoon baking soda
½ teaspoon ground cinnamon
¼ teaspoon ground cloves
½ teaspoon salt
1 cup vegetable shortening
¾ cup granulated sugar
¾ cup packed light brown sugar
2 large eggs, lightly beaten
¼ cup fresh orange juice
1 cup raisins
1 cup flaked coconut

Glaze

¾ cup powdered sugar
1 tablespoon plus 1 teaspoon fresh orange juice
1 teaspoon orange zest, chopped

1 Preheat the oven to 350 degrees. Lightly grease a 15 by 10-inch baking pan.

2 Combine the flour, baking soda, spices, and salt.

3 In a large bowl, cream the vegetable shortening and two sugars. Beat in the eggs. Beat in the orange juice. Gradually blend in the dry ingredients. Fold in the raisins and coconut. Spread the mixture evenly in the prepared baking pan.

4 Bake for 20 to 25 minutes, until lightly colored on top and firm to the touch.

5 Meanwhile, make the glaze: Combine the sugar, orange juice, and orange zest in a small bowl and stir until smooth.

6 Drizzle the glaze over the hot crust. Cool in the pan on a wire rack before cutting into large or small bars.

Raspberry Meringue Bars

Bar Cookies

Yield: 1 to 4 dozen
Total time: 45 minutes

Crust

¾ cup vegetable shortening
¼ cup granulated sugar
2 large eggs, yolks
1½ cups all-purpose flour

Topping

2 large egg whites
½ cup granulated sugar
1 cup almonds, chopped fine
1 cup raspberry puree
1 cup flaked coconut

1 Preheat the oven to 350 degrees. Lightly grease a 13 by 9-inch baking pan.

2 To make the crust, cream the vegetable shortening and sugar in a large bowl. Beat in the egg yolks. Gradually blend in the flour. Spread the dough evenly in the prepared baking pan.

3 Bake for 15 minutes.

4 Meanwhile, make the topping: In a large bowl, beat the egg whites until foamy. Gradually beat in the sugar and beat until the whites hold stiff peaks. Fold in the chopped nuts.

5 Spread the raspberry puree over the hot crust and sprinkle with the coconut. Spread the topping over the coconut.

6 Bake for 20 to 25 minutes longer, or until lightly colored on top and firm to the touch. Cool in the pan on a wire rack before cutting into large or small bars.

ROCKY ROAD BARS

Bar Cookies

YIELD: *1 to 3 dozen*
TOTAL TIME: *40 minutes*

¼ cup all-purpose flour
½ cup walnuts, ground fine
¼ teaspoon baking powder
⅛ teaspoon salt
1 tablespoon vegetable shortening
⅓ cup packed light brown sugar
½ teaspoon vanilla extract

TOPPING
1 cup miniature marshmallows
1 cup (6 ounces) semisweet choco-
    late chips
½ cup walnuts, chopped

1 Preheat the oven to 350
degrees. Lightly grease an 8-inch
square baking pan.

2 Combine the flour, walnuts,
baking powder, and salt.

3 In a large bowl, cream the vegetable shortening and brown
sugar. Beat in the vanilla extract.
Gradually blend in the dry ingredients. Spread the mixture evenly
in the prepared baking pan.

4 Bake for 15 minutes.

5 Meanwhile, to make the topping: In a small bowl, combine
the marshmallows, chocolate
chips, and walnuts and toss to
blend.

6 Spread the topping mixture
evenly over the hot crust. Bake
for 15 to 18 minutes longer, until
the topping is melted and lightly
colored. Cool in the pan on a
wire rack before cutting into
large or small bars.

RUSSIAN TEA COOKIES

Bar Cookies

YIELD: *2 to 3 dozen*
TOTAL TIME: *25 minutes*

2 tablespoons vegetable shortening
¼ cup granulated sugar
2 large egg yolks
1 cup sour milk
2½ cups all-purpose flour

1 Preheat the oven to 350
degrees. Lightly grease a 13 by 9-
inch baking pan.

2 In a large bowl, cream the vegetable shortening and sugar. Beat
in the egg yolks. Beat in the sour
milk. Gradually blend in the
flour. Spread the mixture evenly
into the prepared baking pan.

3 Bake for 10 to 12 minutes, until
lightly colored on top and firm to
the touch. Cool in the pan on a
wire rack before cutting into
large or small bars.

ROCKY ROAD FUDGE BARS

Bar Cookies

YIELD: *1 to 3 dozen*
TOTAL TIME: *40 minutes*

CRUST
½ cup all-purpose flour
½ cup rice flour
1 teaspoon baking powder
1 cup granulated sugar
1 cup almonds, chopped fine
½ cup butter
2 ounces semisweet chocolate, chopped
1 teaspoon almond extract

FILLING
6 ounces cream cheese, at room temperature
¼ cup butter, at room temperature
½ cup powdered sugar
1 large egg
2 tablespoons all-purpose flour
¼ cup almonds, chopped
½ teaspoon almond extract
1 cup (6 ounces) semisweet chocolate chips
2 cups miniature marshmallows

TOPPING
¼ cup butter
2 ounces cream cheese
1 ounce bittersweet chocolate, chopped fine
3½ cups powdered sugar
¼ cup evaporated milk
2 teaspoons amaretto

1 Preheat the oven to 350 degrees. Lightly grease a 13 by 9-inch baking pan.

2 To make the crust, combine the two flours, baking powder, sugar, and almonds in a large bowl.

3 In a double boiler, melt the butter and chocolate over a low heat, stirring until smooth. Remove from heat and stir in the almond extract. Drizzle over the dry ingredients, stirring to form a crumbly dough. Press this evenly into the prepared baking pan.

4 To make the filling, in a medium bowl, beat the cream cheese, butter, powdered sugar, and egg. Beat in the flour. Beat in the almonds and almond extract. Spread the filling evenly over the crust. Sprinkle with the chocolate chips.

5 Bake for 25 to 30 minutes, or until lightly colored. Sprinkle the marshmallows over the top and bake for 2 to 4 minutes longer, until the marshmallows are golden brown.

6 Meanwhile, make the topping: In a medium saucepan, combine the butter, cream cheese, chocolate, and milk and heat over low heat, stirring until smooth. Remove from the heat and stir in the powdered sugar. Stir in the amaretto.

7 Pour the topping over the hot bars and swirl the mixture lightly with a knife. Cool in the pan on a wire rack before cutting into large or small bars.

SEVEN-LAYER COOKIES

Bar Cookies

Yield: *2 to 3 dozen*
Total time: *35 minutes*

1 cup vegetable shortening
1 cup cookie crumbs, such as vanilla wafers or Oreos
1 cup (6 ounces) semisweet chocolate chips
1 cup coconut
1 cup almonds, chopped
1 cup (6 ounces) butterscotch chips
One 14-ounce can sweetened condensed milk

1 Preheat the oven to 350 degrees.

2 Melt the vegetable shortening in a small saucepan and pour into a 13 by 9-inch baking pan. Sprinkle the cookie crumbs over the shortening. Sprinkle the chocolate chips over the crumbs, then sprinkle the coconut over the chocolate chips. Sprinkle the almonds over the coconut and the butterscotch chips over the almonds. Drizzle the condensed milk over the top.

3 Bake for 20 to 30 minutes, until firm to the touch. Cool in the pan on a wire rack before cutting into large or small bars.

SOME-MORE BARS

Bar Cookies

Yield: *1 to 2 dozen*
Total time: *30 minutes*

¾ cup vegetable shortening
⅓ cup granulated sugar
3 cups graham cracker crumbs
2 cups miniature marshmallows
1 cup (6 ounces) semisweet chocolate chips

1 Preheat the oven to 350 degrees. Lightly grease a 13 by 9-inch baking pan.

2 In a large bowl, cream the vegetable shortening and sugar. Gradually blend in the cookie crumbs. Press half of this mixture firmly into the prepared baking pan. Sprinkle the marshmallows and chocolate chips over the top. Crumble over the remaining crumb mix.

3 Bake for 8 to 10 minutes, until firm to the touch. Cool in the pan on a wire rack before cutting into large or small bars.

Spice Bars

Bar Cookies
Yield: *2 to 3 dozen*
Total time: *35 minutes*

1 cup all-purpose flour
¼ cup unsweetened cocoa powder
1 teaspoon baking powder
1 teaspoon ground cinnamon
½ teaspoon ground cloves
½ teaspoon ground allspice
Pinch of salt
¼ cup vegetable shortening
1 cup granulated sugar
3 large eggs
1 teaspoon vanilla extract
½ cup raisins
½ cup walnuts, chopped

1 Preheat the oven to 350 degrees. Lightly grease a 13 by 9-inch baking pan.

2 Combine the flour, cocoa powder, baking powder, spices, and salt.

3 In a large bowl, cream the vegetable shortening and sugar. Beat in the eggs. Beat in the vanilla extract. Gradually blend in the dry ingredients. Fold in the raisins and walnuts. Spread the dough evenly in the prepared baking pan.

4 Bake for 20 to 30 minutes, until the tip of a knife inserted in the center comes out clean. Cool in the pan on a wire rack before cutting into large or small bars.

Baking notes: If you want to frost these bars, do so while they are still warm.

Strawberry Meringue Bars

Bar Cookies
Yield: *3 to 4 dozen*
Total time: *45 minutes*

CRUST
¾ cup vegetable shortening
¼ cup granulated sugar
2 large egg yolks
1½ cups all-purpose flour

FILLING
2 large egg whites
½ cup granulated sugar
1 cup almond, chopped
1 cup strawberry puree
1 cup flaked coconut

1 Preheat the oven to 350 degrees. Lightly grease a 13 by 9-inch square baking pan.

2 To make the crust, cream the vegetable shortening and sugar in a large bowl. Beat in the egg yolks. Gradually blend in the flour. Spread the dough evenly in the bottom of the prepared baking pan.

3 Bake for 15 minutes.

4 Meanwhile, make the topping: In a large bowl, beat the egg whites until foamy. Gradually beat in the sugar and beat in until the whites hold stiff peaks. Fold in the chopped nuts.

5 Spread the strawberry puree over the hot crust and sprinkle with the coconut. Spread the topping over the coconut.

6 Bake for 20 to 25 minutes longer, or until the topping is firm to the touch. Cool in the pan on a wire rack before cutting into large or small bars.

TEATIME FAVORITES

Bar Cookies

YIELD: *2 to 3 dozen*
TOTAL TIME: *50 minutes*

½ cup all-purpose flour
1 cup almonds, ground
2 ounces semisweet chocolate, chopped
½ cup vegetable shortening
1 cup granulated sugar
2 large eggs
½ teaspoon almond extract

1 Preheat the oven to 350 degrees. Lightly grease a 9-inch square baking pan.

2 Combine the flour and almonds.

3 In the top of a double boiler, melt the chocolate and vegetable shortening, stirring until smooth. Remove from the heat and beat in the sugar. Beat in the eggs one at a time, beating vigorously after each addition. Beat in the almond extract. Gradually blend in the dry ingredients. Spread the mixture evenly in the prepared baking pan.

4 Bake for 35 to 40 minutes, or until a toothpick inserted in the center comes out clean. Cool in the pan on a wire rack.

5 Frost the cooled cookies with Vanilla Icing (see Pantry) and cut into large or small bars.

Baking notes: To make a different version of these cookies, bake in a 13 by 9-inch baking pan for 25 to 30 minutes. Let cool in the pan on a wire rack, then use cookie cutters to cut into fancy shapes and frost.

TORTA FREGOLOTTI

Bar Cookies

YIELD: *1 to 3 dozen*
TOTAL TIME: *75 minutes*

2⅔ cups all-purpose flour
1 cup almonds, ground
Pinch of salt
1 cup vegetable shortening
1 cup granulated sugar
1 teaspoon grated lemon zest
2 tablespoons fresh lemon juice
1 tablespoon brandy

1 Preheat the oven to 350 degrees. Lightly grease a 9-inch square baking pan.

2 Combine the flour, almonds, and salt.

3 In a large bowl, cream the vegetable shortening and sugar. Beat in the lemon zest. Gradually blend in the dry ingredients. Measure out ¼ cup of the mixture for the topping and set aside. Beat in the lemon juice and brandy into the remaining dough. Press the dough into the prepared baking pan. Crumble the reserved mixture over the top.

4 Bake for 45 to 50 minutes, until golden brown on top. Cool in the pan on a wire rack before cutting into large or small bars.

TROPICAL BARS

Bar Cookies

YIELD: *2 to 3 dozen*
TOTAL TIME: *35 minutes*

¾ cup all-purpose flour
¾ teaspoon baking powder
½ teaspoon salt
½ cup vegetable shortening
1 cup packed light brown sugar
2 large eggs
½ teaspoon rum
8 ounces canned crushed pineapple, drained
¾ cup flaked coconut

1 Preheat the oven to 350 degrees. Lightly grease a 9-inch square baking pan.

2 Combine the flour, baking powder, and salt.

3 In a large bowl, cream the vegetable shortening and brown sugar. Beat in the eggs and rum. Gradually blend in the dry ingredients. Fold in the pineapple and coconut. Spread the batter evenly in the prepared baking pan.

4 Bake for 25 to 30 minutes, until colored on top. Cool in the pan on a wire rack before cutting into large or small bars.

TROPICAL FRUIT BARS

Bar Cookies

YIELD: *1 to 3 dozen*
TOTAL TIME: *35 minutes*

1¼ cups all-purpose flour
1 teaspoon baking soda
1 tablespoon canola oil
2 large eggs
1 tablespoon pineapple juice, preferrably fresh
1 teaspoon frozen orange juice concentrate, thawed
1¾ cups crushed fresh (or canned) pineapple, drained
1 cup flaked coconut
¾ cup macadamia nuts, chopped

1 Preheat the oven to 350 degrees. Lightly grease a 13 by 9-inch baking pan.

2 Combine the flour and baking soda.

3 In a large bowl, beat the oil and eggs until thick and light-colored. Beat in the pineapple juice and orange juice concentrate. Gradually blend in the dry ingredients. Fold in the pineapple, coconut, and macadamia nuts. Spread the mixture evenly in the prepared baking pan.

4 Bake for 15 to 20 minutes, until lightly colored on top. Cool in the pan on a wire rack before cutting into large or small bars.

WALNUT BARS

Bar Cookies

YIELD: *3 to 4 dozen*
TOTAL TIME: *45 minutes*

CRUST
1⅓ cups all-purpose flour
½ teaspoon baking powder
½ cup packed light brown sugar
⅓ cup vegetable shortening
¼ cup walnuts, chopped

FILLING
3 tablespoons all-purpose flour
½ teaspoon salt
¼ cup packed light brown sugar
2 large eggs
¾ cup dark corn syrup
1 teaspoon vanilla extract
¾ cup walnuts, ground fine

1 Preheat the oven to 350 degrees. Grease a 13 by 9-inch baking pan.

2 To make the crust, combine the flour, baking powder, and brown sugar in a large bowl. Cut in the vegetable shortening until the mixture resembles coarse crumbs. Stir in the walnuts. Spread the mixture evenly in the prepared baking pan.

3 Bake for 10 minutes.

4 Meanwhile, make the filling: Combine the flour and salt.

5 In a medium bowl, beat the brown sugar and eggs until thick and light-colored. Beat in the corn syrup. Beat in the vanilla extract. Gradually blend in the dry ingredients. Pour the filling over the hot crust. Sprinkle the walnuts over the top. Bake for 25 to 30 minutes longer, until the top is firm to the touch. Cool in the pan on a wire rack before cutting into large or small bars.

WALNUT SQUARES I

Bar Cookies

YIELD: *2 to 3 dozen*
TOTAL TIME: *40 minutes*

CRUST
¾ cup vegetable shortening
⅓ cup granulated sugar
2 large egg yolks
1 teaspoon vanilla extract
1½ cups all-purpose flour

FILLING
2 tablespoons all-purpose flour
¼ teaspoon baking powder
¼ teaspoon salt
1½ cups packed light brown sugar
2 large eggs, separated
2 tablespoons evaporated milk
1 teaspoon vanilla extract
1 cup shredded coconut
½ cup walnuts, chopped

1 Preheat the oven to 350 degrees. Lightly grease a 9-inch square baking pan.

2 To make the crust, cream the vegetable shortening and sugar in a medium bowl. Beat in the egg yolks and vanilla extract. Gradually blend in the flour. Press the dough evenly into the prepared baking pan.

3 Bake for 12 minutes.

4 Meanwhile, make the topping: Combine the flour, baking powder, and salt.

5 In a large bowl, beat the brown sugar and eggs. Beat in the milk and vanilla extract. Gradually blend in the dry ingredients. Stir in the coconut and walnuts. Pour the topping over the hot crust. Bake for 20 minutes longer, or until the top is firm to the touch. Cool in the pan on a wire rack before cutting into large or small bars.

WALNUT SQUARES II

Bar Cookies

YIELD: *2 to 3 dozen*
TOTAL TIME: *40 minutes*

CRUST
1 cup all-purpose flour
¼ teaspoon salt
¼ cup vegetable shortening

FILLING
2 tablespoons all-purpose flour
¼ teaspoon salt
¾ cup granulated sugar
2 large eggs
1 teaspoon vanilla extract
2 cups flaked coconut
1 cup walnuts, chopped
Granulated sugar for sprinkling

1 Preheat the oven to 350 degrees. Lightly grease a 9-inch square baking pan.

2 To make the crust, combine the flour and salt in a medium bowl. Cut in the vegetable shortening until the mixture resembles coarse crumbs. Press the mixture evenly into the prepared baking pan.

3 Bake for 12 minutes.

4 Meanwhile, make the topping: Combine the flour and salt.

5 In a medium bowl, beat the sugar and eggs together until thick and light-colored. Beat in the vanilla extract. Gradually blend in the dry ingredients. Stir in the coconut and walnuts.

6 Pour the filling over the hot crust. Bake for 15 minutes longer, or until the topping is set. Sprinkle with granulated sugar and cool in the pan on a wire rack before cutting into large or small bars.

ZUCCHINI BARS I

Bar Cookies

YIELD: *2 to 3 dozen*
TOTAL TIME: *45 minutes*

2½ cups all-purpose flour
1 teaspoon ground cinnamon
½ cup granulated sugar
½ cup vegetable oil
2 large eggs
¾ cup finely chopped zucchini
½ cup mashed, cooked carrots
1 cup pecans, chopped
⅓ cup raisins

1 Preheat the oven to 350 degrees. Lightly grease and flour a 13 by 9-inch baking pan.

2 Combine the flour and cinnamon.

3 In a large bowl, beat the sugar and vegetable oil together. Beat in the eggs one at a time. Beat in the zucchini and carrots. Gradually blend in the dry ingredients. Stir in the pecans and raisins. Spread the batter evenly in the prepared baking pan.

4 Bake for 20 to 25 minutes, until a toothpick inserted in the center comes out clean. Cool in the pan on a wire rack before cutting into large or small bars.

Zucchini Bars II

Bar Cookies

YIELD: *2 to 3 dozen*
TOTAL TIME: *55 minutes*

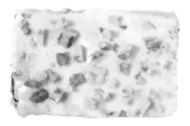

1¾ cups all-purpose flour
1½ teaspoons baking powder
½ teaspoon salt
¾ cup vegetable shortening
½ cup granulated sugar
½ cup packed light brown sugar
2 large eggs
2 teaspoons vanilla extract
2 cups shredded zucchini
¾ cup raisins
½ cup dates, pitted and chopped
½ cup flaked coconut

TOPPING
1 tablespoon vegetable shortening
1 cup powdered sugar
1 tablespoon milk
¼ teaspoon ground cinnamon
1 cup walnuts, chopped

1 Preheat the oven to 350 degrees. Lightly grease a 13 by 9-inch baking pan.

2 Combine the flour, baking powder, and salt.

3 In a large bowl, cream the vegetable shortening and two sugars. Beat in the eggs. Beat in the vanilla extract. Beat in the zucchini. Gradually blend in the dry ingredients. Stir in the raisins, dates, and coconut. Spread the batter evenly in the prepared baking pan.

4 Bake for 30 to 35 minutes, or until a toothpick inserted in the center comes out clean. Cool in the pan on a wire rack.

5 To make the topping, cream the vegetable shortening and powdered sugar in a small bowl. Beat in the milk. Beat in the cinnamon.

6 Spread the topping over the cooled bars and and sprinkle with the chopped walnuts. Cut into large or small bars.

INGREDIENTS

NUTS

Most nuts are available in a variety of forms, including unshelled or shelled, blanched (peeled or skinned) or unblanched, chopped, halved, sliced, or slivered. Cashew nuts are unique in that they are not sold in the shell. Although walnuts, almonds, and pecans are the nuts most commonly used in baking, many other types can result in delicious cookies and baked goods—hazelnuts and hickory nuts, to name just two.

The most inexpensive way to purchase any nuts is in the shell. As a general rule of thumb, one pound of unshelled nuts will equal half a pound of shelled. However, for ease and convenience, many home bakers prefer to buy shelled nuts. Although nuts in the shell stay fresh for a long time, keeping them in the lower part of the refrigerator will prolong their shelf life. Shelled nuts turn rancid quickly and are best kept in airtight containers in the freezer.

The recipes in this book use sliced, slivered, chopped, and ground nuts as well as whole nuts. Chopped means that the nuts are in small corn kernel-size chunks. Ground is when the nut has been reduced to a very coarse, almost powder form.

Almond The fruit of the almond tree can be purchased shelled or unshelled, blanched, or unblanched, slivered, sliced, and chopped. The shell is soft and easy to crack open. Unblanched almonds have a soft brown color; blanched nuts are a pale ivory color.

Black Walnuts Black walnuts were once used extensively in baking recipes, but more widely available English walnuts have replaced them in popularity. Black Walnuts are still preferred by many cooks and bakers; if you come across them, you will want to try baking with these flavorful nuts.

Brazil Nut Although brazil nuts were once available only during the Christmas holiday season, now they are available all year long. They are large nuts most effectively used ground or chopped in cookie recipes.

Cashew This is one of the most popular eating nuts in the world. For baking purposes they are considered a soft nut.

Chestnuts Chestnuts are available fresh in the winter and canned all year around. The best way to prepare fresh chestnuts for cookie recipes is to score them on the bottom and toast them in the oven to loosen their outer shells and skins.

English Walnuts In the United States this is the most

popular nut for cooking purposes. (See Black Walnuts.)

Filbert (See Hazelnuts.)

Hazelnuts The hazelnut, also called filbert, is one of the most flavorful of all nuts. Hazelnuts are far more popular in Europe than in the United States, which is unfortunate in light of the nut's rich taste.

Macadamia Nuts The macadamia nut is one of the most expensive nuts in the world, partly, no doubt, because it takes up to five years before the macadamia tree can start to bear fruit. In addition, macadamia nut trees have never been successfully transplanted to mainland United States. Macadamia nuts have a rich, buttery flavor and are usually toasted in coconut oil.

Peanut This small slick nut (actually a legume), is the most popular eating nut in the United States. Half of the peanut crop is blended into peanut butter, but peanuts turn up in a variety of baked goods, including peanut butter cookies, a perennial favorite.

Pecans Many cooks and bakers prefer the pecan to any other nut; pecans are especially popular in the southern regions of the United States, where they grow profusely.

Pine Nuts Known as *piñon* in Spanish and *pignola* in Italian, the pine nut is usually considered more of an eating nut

than a baking nut, but it works very well in a variety of cookies because of its rich, full flavor.

Pistachio Nuts These nuts, when shelled and toasted work extremely well in cookies because of their complex flavor that melds so well with a variety of spices.

FRUITS

Hundreds of cookie recipes that include fruit in various states—fresh, dried, or frozen.

Dried fruit should be rehydrated before use. The process of rehydration is simply nothing more than soaking the dried fruit in boiling water or another liquid.

Apples Although apples are available throughout the year, they are at their peak in the fall. Cored and sliced dried apples should usually be hydrated before they are used. Applesauce is added to many recipes both to make the cookies softer and to give them a fresh apple taste. Canned apples are not suitable for cookies.

Apricots Fresh apricots are generally available only in season, from May through July. But dried apricots are delicious. Canned apricots tend to be flavorless if used for baking.

Bananas Bananas are available every day of the year. There are two varieties: One is for eating and drying, the other, easily recognizable by its dark skin color, is for cooking. The cooking banana is also smaller than the eating banana. Most home bakers use the eating variety for cooking. Dried banana chips are also available.

Berries Fresh berries including strawberries, blackberries, blueberries, boysenberries, raspberries, black raspberries, are available only in season. We are fortunate that they are always available in the form of jams and preserves which are used in many cookie recipes.

Cherries Fresh cherries are seldom used in cookie baking. They are seldom used as an additive in cookies. (See Glacé/Candied Cherries.)

Dates The fruit of the date palm tree has been used for centuries, as far back as ancient Egypt, as a means of sweetening dishes. Most of the recipes here call for pitted dates.

Figs It is surprising that so few cookie recipes use figs. Fig Newtons are one of this country's most popular cookies.

Lemon Zest Zest and juice of the lemon rind is seldom used in any state other than grated. This adds a pleasing lemon flavor to the cookies in which it is used.

Orange Zest Only the zest and the juice of the orange may be used in baking. The cookies using this zest may have a subtle or strong flavor, depending upon the amounts used.

Peaches Only dried peaches are appropriate for cookies; canned peaches do not hold up under the heat of cooking and become mushy. Fresh peaches may be sliced and layered in bar cookies. Peach puree can be used as a flavor in cookie recipes.

Persimmons A seasonal fruit with a sweet flavor, the persimmon really isn't edible until it is overripe. When the skin starts to turn brown and the pulp inside becomes almost mushy, it is ready to eat or use.

Pineapple Pineapples are readily available all year round, but for baking the canned fruit is most popular because of ease of preparation. It should be well drained before using. Candied pineapple is also good in cookies.

Prunes Dried prunes are used pitted, sliced, or diced in recipes.

SPICES AND HERBS

Allspice These berries, the seeds of the allspice tree, are harvested and sun-dried until they are a deep reddish brown. They are made available whole and ground. Their flavor resembles a soft blend of cloves, cinnamon, and nutmeg (hence the name). Allspice is used to flavor cakes, pies, cookies, and breads. It is especially good in pastries made with fruit.

Anise Anise seeds, or aniseed, are greenish brown with a strong licorice flavor. They are available whole or crushed. Anise seeds are used extensively in cookies and fruit pies, especially in holiday specialties.

Apple pie spice This is a commercial blend of cinnamon, cloves, nutmeg, and some other sweet-type spices. It is used mainly for pies, but in baking, it can be substituted in any recipe that calls for cinnamon or nutmeg.

Caraway seeds Small greenish brown crescent-shaped seeds. Although caraway seeds are perhaps most associated with rye bread, they can be very flavorful in cookies and cakes. The seeds are always sold whole.

Cardamom A member of the ginger family, has a long history; its use has been documented as early as the fourth century B.C. It is available whole or ground. Its sweet flavor makes it a favorite spice in Danish pastries, and it is also used in cakes of all kinds and many cookies. Cardamom is the third most expensive spice in the world.

Cinnamon The bark of a laurel tree; it and its cousin cassia are the two oldest spices known. Both are available in reddish brown rolled sticks or ground. Its sweet pungent taste makes cinnamon one of our most popular spices, used in cakes, pies, cookies, breads, puddings, and other baked goods.

Cloves Cloves are the dried bud of a tropical tree. They have a strong, pungent flavor. Cloves are available both whole and ground; the ground form is used in many cakes, cookies, pies, and fruit desserts; whole cloves are occasionally used in sweets, such as baklava.

Coriander The seed of the coriander, or cilantro plant; it is available whole or ground. The ground seeds are used in cookies, cakes, pies, candies, and other sweets.

Cumin An aromatic seed very similar to caraway seeds in flavor. It is available as seeds or ground.

English spice Commercial blend of several spices with a predominately cinnamon-allspice flavor. It can be used on its own or as a substitute in any baked good that calls for cinnamon, allspice, nutmeg, and cloves.

Fennel seeds These have a mild licorice flavor. They are used in breads and breakfast baked goods.

Ginger Fresh ginger, or ginger root, and the powdered, or dried spice have a hot sweet-spicy flavor. Ginger, both fresh and dried, is used in cakes, breads, cookies, and fruit desserts. Crystallized, or candied, ginger is preserved fresh ginger that has been rolled in sugar.

Mace The lacy outer membrane-like covering of the shell of the nutmeg. Its flavor is sweet, warm, and highly spicy. Mace is usually seen as a powder, but it is also available in flakes or blades.

Mint A perennial herb; peppermint and spearmint are the most popular varieties for flavorings. The dried leaves are available whole, crushed, and powdered.

Nutmeg The seed of the nutmeg tree. It has a sweet-hot taste and a pungent aroma. Available whole or ground, it is used in cakes, pies and cookies. (See Mace.)

Poppy seeds These have a sweet nut-like taste. The tiny black seeds are used extensively to garnish breads, rolls, and cookies.

Sesame seeds Known as benne seeds in the South, these are used to garnish breads, rolls, and cookies. When toasted, the seeds have a very nutty flavor.

Vanilla bean The seed capsule of the vanilla orchid. From this bean is derived the flavoring used to make vanilla extract. The bean itself is used in the preparation of vanilla sugar.

Vanilla extract A liquid derived from the vanilla bean and used extensively as a flavoring in baking and cooking. Synthetic vanillas are available for a lesser price.

CHOCOLATE

For our purposes, cocoa powder, unsweetened chocolate, semisweet or bittersweet chocolate, chocolate syrup, and chocolate chips are the foundations of the world of the chocolate cookie.

Unsweetened chocolate means baker's-style chocolate. Baker's-style chocolate is bitter chocolate and is the base for most other chocolate products. It can be found in the supermarket in the baking section in 14- to 16-ounce packages. The chocolate is divided into small squares, and each square weighs one ounce.

Semisweet chocolate, sometimes called bittersweet, is packaged the same way, too, but there is a wide variety of imported bittersweet or semisweet chocolate available as well.

Cocoa is the powdered form of chocolate. For baking, use unsweetened cocoa powder, not the sweet cocoa for drinking.

Milk chocolate has long been a favorite of the candy-loving public. But milk chocolate can't be used interchangeably with other types of chocolate in most recipes.

White chocolate has gained in popularity in recent years. White chocolate is not actually chocolate, because it contains no chocolate liquor. It is cocoa butter with sugar and milk added.

Many of the recipes in this book call for melting chocolate. It isn't difficult if you follow a few separate rules. Chocolate should always be melted over low heat in an absolutely dry pan. *Dry* is the key word. When you are melting chocolate by itself, the slightest drop of liquid or moisture can cause the chocolate to seize, or to become stiff and lumpy. (If you are adding other ingredients, the general rule of thumb is one tablespoon of liquid to one ounce of chocolate. It is the minute amounts of liquid that cause the trouble.) *For this reason, the pan melting the chocolate in should never be covered* because condensation may form on the lid and drip into the chocolate. If chocolate should seize, you often can save it by stirring in one teaspoon per ounce of chocolate of vegetable shortening. (*Do not use butter or margarine.*)

Chocolate burns easily, so using a double boiler is recommended. If you don't have one, you can put the chocolate in a heatproof cup and place it in a saucepan partially filled with water, over very low heat. (Milk chocolate should be melted at a lower temperature than unsweetened or semisweet chocolate.) Then stir the chocolate occasionally, until it is smooth.

A microwave oven also works well for melting. Consult your owner's manual for instructions with your particular microwave.

MISCELLANEOUS

Candied Beads *(Silver or Gold Balls)* Candied beads or balls have been around for many years. They are used more for decoration, especially for holiday cookies.

Candied Citron The citron is rarely available in the United States. At a time when oranges and lemons were not readily available, its peel was used in place of other members of the citrus family.

Chocolate Candies Usually the chocolate candies used in cookies are of the wafer type, such as mints or pralines.

Chocolate Chips In the early 1900s Ruth Wakefield, who worked at the The Tollhouse Inn in Massachusetts, chopped a baker's style bar of chocolate and added the pieces to a batch of cookie dough, making the first chocolate chip cookies. Because of that woman's inventiveness, a whole industry developed. In addition to semisweet chocolate chips, there are now butterscotch, peanut butter, and white chocolate used in baking.

Glacé/Candied Cherries This form of dried cherries sweetened with sugar are used diced up in cookie recipes, and as decorative toppings on cookies.

Jelly Candies Like other candies, they are used more for a decoration than for flavor. Jelly candies and gumdrops are used whole, or are chopped and added to the dough.

Jimmies These candies come in chocolate or rainbow colors, and are a great addition to many cookies.

Sugar Crystals These are sprinkled on the cookies after they have been formed and or baked. Like candy beads, they are added to a cookie strictly for decoration. They come colored or white.

FLAVORINGS

Using liqueur or brandy in cookie recipes opens up a whole new world of flavoring possibilities, while keeping your costs at a minimum.

Each liqueur or brandy listed below is as economical as a small 1- or 2-ounce bottle of vanilla extract. If the products are kept well-corked or capped, there is little chance of them going bad before you have time to use them. Also, most of the imitation flavoring products have little or no alcohol, and have a better chance of going bad than the flavored liqueur. There is a world of flavoring out there in addition to those you see in the grocery store.

ALTERNATIVE FLAVORINGS

Liqueur/Brandy	Flavor
Abisante	anise and herb
Advokaat	eggnog
Ari	plum
Amaretto	apricot almond
Amaretto/Cognac	amaretto
Ambrosia Liqueur	caramel
Amer Picon	orange
Anisette	anise
Antioqueno	anise
Apry	apricot
Arak	rum
Ashanti Gold	chocolate
Averna Liqueur	herbal
Irish Cream	fresh cream
Baitz Island Creme	almond
	coconut
	chocolate
Barenjäger	honey
Benedictine	herbal
Blackberry Brandy	blackberry
Boggs Cranberry	cranberry
Bucca di Amore	anise
	herb
	spices
Cafe Brizard	coffee
Cafe orange	coffee & orange
Cafe Lolita	coffee
Campari	orange/caramel
	vanilla
Carmella	vanilla
Chambord Liqueur	raspberry
	fruit
	herb
	honey
CherriStock	cherry
Cherry Brandy	cherry

Liqueur/Brandy	Flavor
Choclair	chocolate/coconut
Cinnamon Schnapps	cinnamon
Club Raki	licorice
Coffee Brandy	coffee
Coffee Liqueur	coffee
Cranberria	cranberry
Conticream	chocolate cream
Crème de Almond	almond
Crème de Banana	banana
Crème de Cacao	chocolate
Crème de Cafe	coffee
Crème de Cassis	black currant
Crème de Framboise	raspberry
Crème de Menthe	peppermint
Crème de Prunella	plum
Crème de Strawberry	strawberry
Cuarenta Y Tres	vanilla
Droste Bittersweet	bittersweet chocolate
Fraise des Bois	wild strawberry
Ginger Brandy	ginger
Ginger Schnapps	ginger
Kümmel	caraway
Lemonier	lemon
Lemonique	tart lemon
Mandarinette	tangerines
Mandarino	tangy orange
	cherry
Marron Liqueur	chestnut
Midori	honeydew melon
Paso Fino Rum	rum
Peach Brandy	peach
Pear William	Anjou pear
Peppermint Schnapps	peppermint
Peter Herring	cherry
Praline Liqueur	vanilla & pecan
Spearmint Schnapps	spearmint
Straretto	strawberry

PANTRY

These recipes are standard frostings, icings, fillings, and bar cookie crusts. They are referenced for use throughout the main cookie recipe text.

FROSTINGS AND ICINGS

RICH BUTTERCREAM
YIELD: 2 TO 2½ CUPS
½ cup butter, at room temperature
3½ cups powdered sugar
⅛ teaspoon salt
1 large egg yolk
About 1 tablespoon milk

In a large bowl, cream the butter. Beat in the powdered sugar. Beat in the salt and egg yolk. Add just enough milk to make a spreadable frosting. Flavor the buttercream with any of the following suggestions, or add a flavoring of your own choice. (Note: Buttercream frostings have a tendency to soften during hot weather. If this happens, beat in a little cornstarch to bring the mixture back to the desired consistency.)

For the following flavored buttercreams use the Rich Buttercream recipe with the added flavorings.

VANILLA BUTTERCREAM
Add 1 teaspoon vanilla extract.

ALMOND BUTTERCREAM
Add 1 teaspoon almond extract or Amaretto.

ORANGE BUTTERCREAM
Add 1 teaspoon orange liqueur.

LEMON BUTTERCREAM
Add 1 teaspoon lemon extract.

RUM BUTTERCREAM
Add 1 teaspoon rum.

BRANDY BUTTERCREAM
Add 1 teaspoon brandy or cognac.

COCOA BUTTERCREAM
Add 1 teaspoon crème de cacao.

RASPBERRY BUTTERCREAM
Add 1 teaspoon raspberry liqueur.

COFFEE BUTTERCREAM
Add 1 teaspoon strong coffee.

APRICOT BUTTERCREAM
Add 1 teaspoon apricot brandy.

DECORATING BUTTERCREAM
YIELD: 4 TO 4½ CUPS
2 cups vegetable shortening
4 cups powdered sugar
1 to 2 large egg whites
Pinch of salt
Vanilla or other flavoring to taste

In a large bowl, cream the shortening. Gradually beat in the powdered sugar. Beat in the egg whites. Beat in the salt. Beat in the flavoring. Remember that a little flavoring goes a long way; think in terms of drops, not spoonfuls. (Note: Buttercream frostings have a tendency to soften during hot weather. If this happens, beat in a little cornstarch to bring the mixture back to the desired consistency.)

CHOCOLATE FROSTING I
YIELD: 2 TO 2½ CUPS
5⅓ tablespoon butter, at room temperature
½ cup Dutch process unsweetened cocoa powder
Pinch of salt
3 tablespoons boiling water
1½ cups powdered sugar, or more if necessary

In a large bowl, cream the butter. Beat in the cocoa. Add the salt and boiling water, stirring until you have a smooth paste. Beat in the powdered sugar and beat until the frosting reaches a spreadable consistency. If it seems too thick, add a few drops of water; if it seems too thin, add a little more powdered sugar.

CHOCOLATE FROSTING II

YIELD: 1 TO 1½ CUPS

1½ ounces unsweetened chocolate, chopped

1 tablespoon butter, at room temperature

¼ cup sour cream

½ teaspoon vanilla extract

1½ cups powdered sugar, or more if necessary

Melt the chocolate in a double boiler over low heat, stirring until smooth. Remove from the heat and beat in the butter and sour cream. Beat in the vanilla extract. Gradually beat in the powdered sugar and beat until the frosting reaches a spreadable consistency. If it seems too thick, add a few drops of water; if it seems too thin, add a little more powdered sugar.

CHOCOLATE FROSTING III

YIELD: 1 TO 1¼ CUPS

1 cup (6 ounces) semisweet chocolate chips

2 teaspoons boiling water

2 tablespoons light corn syrup

2 teaspoons strong brewed coffee

Place the chocolate chips in a small bowl and pour the boiling water over them. Start beating and add the corn syrup and coffee. If it seems too thick, add a few drops of water; if it seems too thin, add a little more powdered sugar.

DARK CHOCOLATE ICING

YIELD: 1 TO 1½ CUPS

6 ounces unsweetened chocolate, chopped

2 tablespoons butter, at room temperature

1 teaspoon vanilla extract

⅛ teaspoon salt

2 cups powdered sugar

⅓ cup milk

Melt the chocolate in the top of a double boiler over low heat, stirring until smooth. Remove from the heat and beat in the butter. Beat in the vanilla and salt. Gradually beat in the powdered sugar. Beat in just enough milk to make a spreadable frosting.

VANILLA ICING I

YIELD: ABOUT ½ CUP

½ cup powdered sugar

1 tablespoon water

Put the powdered sugar in a small bowl. Beat in the water and continue beating until the icing reaches the desired consistency. If the icing is too thick, add more water; if it is too thin, add more powdered sugar.

VANILLA ICING II

YIELD: 2 TO 2¼ CUPS

3 cups powdered sugar

⅓ cup evaporated milk

1½ teaspoons vanilla extract

Put 1 cup of the powdered sugar in a medium bowl and beat in the milk and vanilla extract. Gradually beat in the remaining 2 cups powdered sugar and continue beating until the icing reaches the desired consistency. If the icing is too thick, add more water; if it is too thin, add more powdered sugar.

GREEN CRÈME DE MENTHE ICING

YIELD: 2 TO 2¼ CUPS

Use the same ingredients as in Vanilla Icing II, except replace the vanilla extract with 1½ teaspoons green crème de menthe liqueur, and follow the same instructions.

LEMON SUGAR ICING

YIELD: ABOUT ½ CUP

½ cup powdered sugar

1 teaspoon fresh lemon juice

1 tablespoon water

Put the powdered sugar in a small bowl. Beat in the lemon

juice and water and continue beating until the icing reaches the desired consistency. If the icing is too thick add more water; if it is too thin add more powdered sugar.

Baking notes: For a tarter lemon taste, use lemon extract in place if the lemon juice.

ALMOND CREAM FILLING
YIELD: 1¾ TO 2 CUPS

Combine 1½ cups heavy cream, 1 cup powdered sugar, and 1 cup finely ground almonds in a medium saucepan and bring to a boil, stirring frequently. Cook, stirring constantly, until the mixture has thickened and reduced to about 2 cups. Remove from the heat and stir in 2 tablespoons Amaretto.

APPLE FILLING
YIELD: 2½ TO 3 CUPS

Peel, core, and thinly slice 5 apples. Place them in a large saucepan and add just enough water to cover. Bring to a boil and cook, stirring, occasionally, until the apples are very soft. Drain well and transfer to a medium bowl. Mash the apples with a wooden spoon or potato masher. Add ½ cup powdered sugar, 2 tablespoons Amaretto, 1 tablespoon fresh lemon juice, 1 tablespoon grated lemon zest, and ⅛ teaspoon ground nutmeg and stir until well blended.

CHOCOLATE CHEESECAKE FILLING
YIELD: 3 TO 3½ CUPS

In a large bowl, combine 1 pound room-temperature cream cheese, ¾ cup unsweetened cocoa powder, and ½ cup granulated sugar and beat until smooth and creamy. Beat in 4 large eggs one at a time, beating well after each addition. Beat in 2 tablespoons chocolate syrup.

COCONUT-PECAN FILLING
YIELD: 2½ TO 3 CUPS

Combine 1 cup evaporated milk, 3 large egg yolks, 1 cup granulated sugar, ½ cup vegetable shortening, and 1 teaspoon coconut flavoring in a large saucepan and cook over medium-low heat, stirring, until thick, 10 to 12 minutes. (Do not let the mixture boil.) Remove from the heat and stir in 1 cup flaked coconut and 1 cup chopped pecans. Let cool.

LEMON FILLING
YIELD: 2 TO 2½ CUPS

In a large bowl, combine 4 large eggs and 2 cups granulated sugar and beat until thick and light-colored. Beat in ⅓ cup all-purpose flour, 6 tablespoons lemon juice concentrate, and 1 teaspoon grated lemon zest. (This filling is to be poured over a partially baked crust and then baked until set and firm to the touch.)

PUMPKIN CHEESECAKE FILLING
YIELD: 3¼ TO 4 CUPS

In a large bowl, combine 11 ounces room-temperature cream cheese and ⅔ cups granulated sugar and beat until smooth and creamy. Beat in 16 ounces solid-pack pumpkin, 3 large eggs, 1½ teaspoons ground cinnamon, and 1 teaspoon vanilla extract (or another flavoring of your choice).

VANILLA SUGAR
YIELD: 1½ TO 2 CUPS

Rinse a vanilla bean in cold water and dry thoroughly with paper towels. Put 1½ to 2 cups sugar in a pint jar, add the vanilla bean, and shake well. Let stand for a few days, shaking the jar occasionally, before using the flavored sugar. Replenish the jar as you use it.

Here are almost twenty-one ideas for bar cookie crusts. (These are to be spread or patted into the bottom of a baking pan and partially baked before a topping or filling is spread over the crust and baked until done.) But, in fact, these should provide you with ideas for dozens of crusts. Any of these combinations can be varied according to your personal taste. For example, in a recipe that calls for all-purpose flour, you could substitute whole wheat flour, rice flour, or even buckwheat flour for some (usually no more than about a quarter) of the white flour. Or use vegetable shortening in place of butter in a crust. Or replace granulated sugar with brown sugar or raw sugar. Use your favorite nuts in any nut crust, or your favorite cookies in a crumb crust. And of course you can also change the flavoring, substituting another extract for vanilla, adding a liqueur, and so forth.

Use your imagination, but do keep one guideline in mind. If you are changing the crust in a favorite recipe, be sure to replace it with a similar crust, one that "matches" the filling or topping as in the original recipe. A filling that is very runny before it is baked, for example, needs the right kind of crust to support the unbaked filling. A crust that takes a long time to bake will not be cooked if combined with a topping that takes only minutes to bake. Keep baking times in mind when you are experimenting. Have fun!

See Bar Cookies in the text for basic procedures for combining particular ingredients to make a crust.

1
1 cup all-purpose flour
½ cup powdered sugar
6 tablespoons butter
1 tablespoon heavy cream

2
3 cups all-purpose flour
1 cup granulated sugar
1 cup butter
4 large eggs, separated
2 large egg yolks
½ teaspoon salt

3
16 graham crackers, crushed
½ cup granulated sugar
¼ cup butter

4
1 cup all-purpose flour
¾ cup granulated sugar
½ cup butter
⅓ cup milk
1 large egg
¾ teaspoon Amaretto

5
1 cup all-purpose flour
½ cup butter
¼ teaspoon salt

6
24 gingersnaps, crushed
¼ cup powdered sugar
½ cup canola oil

7
2 cups all-purpose flour
¼ cup granulated sugar

½ cup butter
¼ cup walnuts, ground fine

8

1½ cups whole wheat flour
¾ cup butter
2 tablespoons granulated sugar

9

1¼ cups all-purpose flour
½ cup vegetable shortening
¼ teaspoon salt
3 tablespoons ice water

10

1 cup all-purpose flour
½ cup powdered sugar
½ cup butter
½ cup shredded coconut
¼ teaspoon salt

11

1½ cups all-purpose flour
⅔ cup granulated sugar
½ cup butter
3 large egg yolks
2 tablespoons milk

12

1⅓ cups all-purpose flour
½ cup packed light brown sugar
⅓ cup butter
½ teaspoon baking powder
½ cup almonds, chopped

13

2 cups all-purpose flour
3 tablespoons powdered sugar
2 large egg yolks
1 teaspoon instant coffee
   crystals
1 tablespoon water

14

1⅓ cups crushed gingersnaps
¼ cup packed light brown sugar
2 tablespoons butter
3½ ounces macadamia nuts,
   ground fine
1½ teaspoons crystallized ginger, chopped

15

1 cup all-purpose flour
¼ cup light brown sugar
6 tablespoons butter
½ cup pecans, chopped fine
¼ teaspoon salt

16

1⅓ cup all-purpose flour
½ cup packed light brown sugar
⅓ cup butter
½ teaspoon baking powder
¼ cup hazelnuts, ground fine

17

1 cup all-purpose flour
½ cup packed light brown sugar
½ cup butter
¼ teaspoon ground cloves
½ teaspoon ground ginger
¼ teaspoon ground nutmeg

18

1½ cups all-purpose flour
½ cup butter
¼ teaspoon salt
2½ tablespoons warm water

19

2 cups all-purpose flour
¼ cup granulated sugar
½ cup butter
½ cup walnuts, ground fine

20

2 cups all-purpose flour
2 cups packed light brown sugar
1 cup butter

21

1 cup all-purpose flour
¾ cup packed light brown sugar
⅓ cup butter
2 large egg yolks
1 cup shredded coconut